ALLEN BREED SERIES

The Allen Breed Series examines horse and pony breeds from all over the world, using a broad interpretation of what a breed is: whether created by the environment where it originally developed, or by man for a particular purpose, selected for its useful characteristics, or for its appearance, such as colour. It includes all members of the horse family, and breeds with closed or protected stud books as well as breeds and types still developing.

Each book in the Allen Breed Series examines the history and development of the breed, its characteristics and use, and its current position in Britain, together with an overview of the breed in America and worldwide. More difficult issues are also tackled, such as particular problems associated with the breed, and such controversies as the effect of the show ring on working breeds. The breed societies and their role in modern breeding policies are discussed.

BOOKS IN THE SERIES

The Appaloosa
The Arabian Horse
The Coloured Horse and Pony
The Fell Pony
The Hackney
The Haflinger
The Hanoverian
The Irish Draught Horse
The Morgan Horse
The Mule
The Quarter Horse
The Trakehner
The Welsh Mountain Pony

The Haflinger

The Haflinger and handler in their national costume.

ALLEN BREED SERIES

The Haflinger

Helen Deverill

J. A. Allen

London

British Library Cataloguing in Publication Data
A catalogue record for this book is available from the British Library

ISBN 0–85131–644–1

Published in Great Britain in 1996 by
J. A. Allen & Company Limited
1 Lower Grosvenor Place
London SW1W 0EL

Series editor Elizabeth O'Beirne-Ranelagh
Book production Bill Ireson
Printed in Great Britain by Redwood Books, Trowbridge, Wiltshire

Contents

		Page
ACKNOWLEDGEMENTS		ix
1	Introduction	1
2	Origins of the breed	5
3	Development from 1918 to the present day	12
4	Breeding and bloodlines	25
5	Care, competition and training	40
6	Haflingers in Britain	57
7	Haflingers worldwide	82
8	And so to the future	93
BIBLIOGRAPHY		98
INDEX OF HORSES' NAMES		99

Front cover: Brownbread Story at home in the snow (*Photo: Elisabeth Brotherton*)
Endpapers: The Oxnead 'gang', 1987 (*Photo: Elisabeth Brotherton*)

Acknowledgements

I wish to thank the following people for their help and those who provided photographs and drawings and gave their permission to publish them. Jenny Bickerton, photograph on page 79; Elisabeth Brotherton, cover photograph, and photographs on pages 2, 19, 26, 41, 44, 45, 46, 47, 49, 50, 51, 62, 63, 66, 71, 73, 77, 78, 83, 85; Lesley Brown, photograph on page 48; Dominic Coleman, map on page 6 and drawing on page 27; Tom Crane, photograph on page 64; Jane Dotchin, photographs on pages 53, 54; Ron Duggins, photograph on page 70; Alex Fell, photograph on page 94; June Gillis, drawings on pages 13, 29, 39, 56, 97 and photographs on pages 65, 96; Pat Harrison; Haflinger Society of Great Britain; Eve Paxton-Brown, photographs on pages 90, 91; Helen Robbins, photograph on page 61; Anne Rolinson, photographs on pages 60, 70; and Herr Otto and Herr Hannes Schweisgut, frontispiece and photographs on pages 3, 8, 9, 10, 16, 22, 23, 31, 32, 33, 34, 35, 36, 60.

Introduction

The Austrians call the Haflinger a 'leisure-time sport horse', a rather quaint phrase which probably sums up its versatility as accurately as anything else could. It has also been referred to as a 'blonde bombshell' and a horse that conquers everyone's heart. These comments too are very appropriate to the Haflinger's spectacular looks and loving temperament. Once one has seen a Haflinger, it is rarely forgotten, being easily identifiable by its uniformity of colour and type, while its kindly nature and engaging character endears it to old and young alike.

The Haflinger originated from a breed of small mountain horses which had roamed the area south of the Alps for many centuries. This small horse gradually developed most of the characteristics which are present in the Haflinger today: hardiness, strength and surefootedness in particular. Some 120 years ago, in the South Tyrol, attempts were made to improve this native breed by crossing some of the mares with a half Arabian stallion, El'Bedavi XXII. The result was Folie, a Haflinger stallion who is considered to be the founding father of the Haflinger breed as it is known today. Although the breed has been much more scientifically developed for the last seventy or so years, selective breeding has not detracted in any way from the native hardiness which had previously evolved over the centuries when the horses roamed wild in the mountains. In fact, if anything, it has led to the emphasis of the best traits and to some uniformity of the breed, which is essentially still a mountain pony.

The Austrian breeding standards which currently apply have not changed significantly in over seventy years, apart from a brief period during the Second World War when controlled breeding had to be temporarily abandoned. This led to a slightly different type of Haflinger emerging for a short time between the late 1930s and the early 1950s. Despite the fact that the Haflinger was bred initially as a working horse, the combination of native hardiness, spirit and elegance has led to its development as an all-round horse for a very wide variety of equestrian activities.

Although Haflingers are frequently referred to as horses, the original German *Haflingerpferde* translating literally as Haflinger horses, they are, strictly speaking, ponies. Their size ranges from 13 hh to 14.3 hh and they have an attractive, striking appearance. The colour is always chestnut (although this may range from a very pale shade of gold to a dark chocolate colour) with profuse and flowing flaxen or white manes and tails. They have strong bodies with comparatively short legs, and excellent bone. The current breeding policy is showing a return to producing the better quality and taller animals of the earlier days, rather than those of minimum height and

1

Brownbread Story – freedom in the snow.

very chunky build which were bred in the middle part of the twentieth century for pack work. Haflingers today are becoming increasingly sought after as riding animals. They are up to considerable weight for both riding and driving and possess a superb quiet temperament which is very carefully guarded and considered to be as important an attribute as good conformation.

A strict, some may even say draconian, breeding regime has been developed in Austria. Only the very best animals are permitted to be used for breeding, which is mainly controlled by the State. Those mares which do not meet the high standards required may often end up on the meat market. Colts not meeting the criteria have to be gelded, after which they may be used as working animals; otherwise they too may be used for meat. However, dedicated application of this policy has ensured that the pedigree Haflinger retains uniformity and excellence of quality, and has not allowed undesirable characteristics to infiltrate the breed. It would be very easy to end up with a breed of brownish, nondescript mountain ponies in just a few generations if that policy were allowed to lapse.

The modern bloodlines can all be traced back through seven stallion lines to the first Haflinger stallion (Folie), the result of the original cross between the half Arab stallion and the Tyrolean mare. These bloodlines are very important and will be explained in greater detail later in the book. Each has slightly different characteristics and could affect the choice of a horse, depending on the purpose for which it was being purchased.

Haflingers are very good doers and do not need large quantities of lush grass or hard food. However, they are very greedy and fencing needs to be especially secure

Mares and foals on the high pasture in the Tyrol in August.

because they are always on the lookout for something better on the other side! They also need shelter as, although they can withstand very low temperatures, the combination of cold, wet and windy weather does affect them, despite their being a hardy breed. In their native Austria, during the long winter months they normally live in stables which are situated underneath the family farmhouse. In the summer they are put out to graze on the High Pastures or *Alms*, as they are known in Austria.

The breed is now well established in many different countries and on all five continents. They have been found to adapt well to extremes of climate, with the help of a little basic commonsense in the methods of care. Haflingers were first imported into Great Britain in the 1960s. In the early 1970s the Haflinger Society of Great Britain was formed under the auspices of the Duchess of Devonshire, to ensure that the original standards of the breed continued to be met and therefore to be perpetrated. The British society retains close links with Austria and is a member of the World Haflinger Federation.

Today the ponies are used for many different equestrian activities including endurance riding, dressage, cross country, hunting, hacking, driving, trekking, and Riding for the Disabled. Their gentle nature makes them ideal as family ponies, for although they can sometimes be too strong off the leading rein for small children, they are equally suitable for both teenagers and adults and their versatility gives them the ability to undertake whatever activity their owners choose to participate in.

The following chapters will look more closely at the origins of the breed and its background in its native Austria; its conformation and characteristics; bloodlines and development; its lifestyle, care and training; worldwide distribution and in particular Haflingers in Great Britain; and finally to consider the future of the breed and its place in the modern world.

Origins of the breed

Although a great deal of research has been carried out in the endeavour to ascertain how long the Haflinger type of Tyrolean Mountain pony has been in existence, and in particular to try and pinpoint when and where it first appeared, the exact origins of that breed still remain uncertain, although it is known that similar ponies have roamed the mountains for a number of centuries.

The native home of the Haflinger is generally considered to be the Salten-Mölten Plateau in the Etsch (Adige) Valley of the South Tyrol (see map). Although this was still part of the Austro-Hungarian Empire in the early days of the modern Haflinger's development, the South Tyrol had to be relinquished to Italy in 1919 after the end of the First World War, causing more than a little hostility between the Austrians and the Italians and resulting in conflicting ideas on the importance of the Haflinger. Nevertheless, it was the Austrians who contributed most to continuing the development of the breed, despite this geographical technicality of the Haflinger homeland now being in Italy. The actual name, Haflinger, is derived from the small village of Hafling, near Meran (Merano) in the South Tyrol.

It has been established for a long time, from the evidence of prehistoric artefacts and Celtic graves, that man was an early settler in the area. Horse breeding is also thought to have begun at an early stage, since the existence of horses was recorded in the Etsch Valley as far back as 1282. Late medieval documents also mention 'a race of small mountain horses, south of the Alps'. Other documents confirm that while the Norican horse, which was a heavier draught type of breed, was found in early times in the North Tyrol, there was a lighter breed of horses with indications of Oriental blood evolving in the south from the Middle Ages onwards. These lighter horses were probably the ancestors of the Haflinger. It is now thought likely that the Oriental bloodlines were introduced into European breeding stock during the various Asian invasions of Europe. These horses then continued to breed, both in the wild and with some help from man, for more than 500 years, during most of which time the South Tyrol belonged to the Austro-Hungarian Empire.

In early times the inhabitants of the South Tyrol preferred their smaller, lighter horses because the difficult and mountainous nature of the territory made it necessary to have surefooted and nimble horses to ride over precarious ground. Later on, however, transport routes improved and a need emerged for a stronger and larger horse for draught purposes. This probably led to crossbreeding with the Noricans, which produced a somewhat heavier type of animal (although still lighter than the Norican)

5

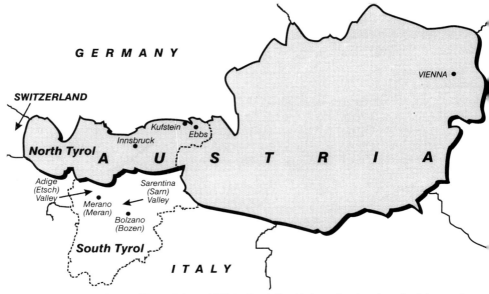

The homeland of the Haflinger. Prior to 1919 the South Tyrol belonged to Austria; today it is part of Italy.

which became established as the native Tyrolean type of mountain pony and the fore-runner of today's Haflinger.

The development of the Haflinger as we know it today began in 1874 with the birth of the stallion Folie, sired by the half Arab stallion El'Bedavi XXII and out of one of the lighter types of Tyrolean mare. This injection of Arabian blood improved the native type enormously, but without taking away the essential characteristics which were demanded of the breed. The progeny of El'Bedavi XXII formed the foundation stock of the modern Haflinger breed. Other Oriental stallions were also tried at this time, but it was found for some reason that the desired traits for the Haflinger were missing from these lines, so breeding with these other stallions was discontinued.

Folie became the first registered Haflinger stallion and is thus considered to be the founder of the modern breed. He was raised by a man named Rochus Eberhofer who was a well-known breeder of the period and who considered that this stallion showed

6

great potential. Someone else who also recognised that the Haflinger had possibilities at this time was Count Moritz von Leon, a local man of status with considerable influence, who was the owner of Fragsburg Castle near Meran. He was sufficiently impressed with the breed that in 1875 he persuaded officials from the Austrian Imperial Ministry of Agriculture to visit the region and in particular to inspect the stud where Folie was kept. These officials were very impressed with the animals they saw and decided to initiate a specific state-controlled Haflinger breeding programme. Once this was implemented, Haflinger stallions which were selected as suitable for breeding purposes were registered in consecutive order of birth, thus establishing the male lines fairly firmly from an early date. Unfortunately in those early days little attention was paid to the mare lines. Nevertheless, the foundations of selective Haflinger breeding had been laid.

However, another two decades were to pass before the true pioneer of purebred Haflinger breeding appeared on the scene. This was a Count Huyn, who had been a Major in the Austrian Army before being appointed as Director of the state-controlled National Stallion Depot in 1897, a position which he held until 1906. After that he became the government Equine Breeding Inspector for a further four years. Count Huyn had strong ties with the Tyrol and he used the position and influence he gained as National Stallion Depot Director to encourage and assist in the breeding of horses native to that area, thereby giving the Haflinger a considerable advantage.

When Count Huyn first assumed his appointment in 1897, he embarked on an inspection tour of all the studs throughout western Austria. The result of this tour was a somewhat critical report of the haphazard and uncontrolled breeding which was taking place at the time in the South Tyrol. Count Huyn's recommendation was that an organised breeding programme should be developed to ensure that the Haflinger, which by now had become an essential possession of the Tyrolean farmers, would be properly established and continue to exist as a pure breed in the future. This report became the basis for the well-planned and carefully controlled breeding programme which still exists today.

To begin with, a number of the best Haflinger colts were chosen and purchased from studs in the South Tyrol by Count Huyn in his position as a government official. They were then transferred to the state-controlled studs at Ossiach in Carinthia, Stadl-Paura in Upper Austria and Piber in Styria in order to establish breeding over a wider area. These first Haflinger colts which were selectively dispersed became the foundation stock for the new breeding programme. The Austrians regard them today as being extremely important, as all bloodlines can be traced back through one or more of these animals to Folie. Their names were 32 Campi, liz. 252/233 Hafling, liz.

7

A surefooted pony is needed when it comes to crossing a swift running mountain stream with a heavy load.

42 Mandl, 54 Genter and 291 Jenner. (All Austrian Haflingers are identified by their stud number as well as the name, since the same name may be repeated down the generations.)

In 1899 the Austrian government was offering a subsidy to encourage horse breeding, so a number of high quality Haflinger fillies were then selected on its behalf to establish a government-assisted Haflinger breeding programme. Around the same time, the Austrian Ministry of Agriculture directed that between six and ten of the best Haflinger colts and fillies available should be purchased annually from the South Tyrol homeland. The colts were taken to the National Foal Centre at Ossiach where they spent their first four years. They wintered at the Centre and spent their summers on the *Alms* or High Pastures at Piber. Even in summer, the climate can be severe and the young Haflingers not only had to adapt to the weather, but also to differences in altitude, all of which helped them to develop into hardier adults. Early training consisted of regular handling to teach the youngsters to trust humans, thus preparing them for breaking and schooling at a later date. At four years old those which were considered to have stallion potential were transferred to the stud at Stadl-Paura, where they underwent further training before being dispersed to stand at studs throughout the country. Those which did not reach the high standards required for breeding were given to the Army, where they were used as pack animals. The fillies spent the first three years of their lives at the *Tschaufenhof* in South Tyrol, after which time they were assigned to approved breeders free of charge. This was in order to encourage private breeders, many of whom were farmers, to participate specifically in the organised breeding of selected Haflingers, which they might not otherwise have done.

The first breed society was formed in 1904 at Mölten by a group of South Tyrolean breeders, encouraged by the Imperial Ministry of Agriculture, and was known as the

Young Haflingers at play at the *Fohlenhof*.

Haflinger Breeders Co-operative. The aims of that organisation were general improvement of Haflinger breeding procedures by using only the best quality stallions and conscientiously practising selective breeding. Special emphasis was put on promoting purebreeding, the establishment and maintenance of a stallion register and a stud book for the mares, and providing information and instruction on breeding and raising the animals, especially to those outside the Co-operative. The Austrian government continued to show enthusiastic support for the breed and donated prize

A Haflinger works hard for his owner, logging in the mountains.

money and medals to the Breeders Co-operative Annual Show. The government also continued to subsidise breeding by paying a premium for every animal which had been raised on the *Alms* during summer, since this was considered to be a very important part of the young Haflingers' development.

It can thus be seen that during the latter part of the nineteenth century and the early years of the twentieth century Haflinger breeding progressed steadily in an organised manner. It also spread further afield until Haflingers were being bred over a considerable area of Austria, including becoming well established in the North Tyrol. This was fortunate for the Austrians in their later work in developing the modern Haflinger, in light of what was to happen after the First World War when Austria lost the South Tyrol to Italy as part of the peace settlement.

At this time the Haflinger was being used more as a working horse than a riding animal. Haflingers were a major asset of the Tyrolean farmers for whom they carried out all types of farmwork, often being considered as 'part of the family'. They were also greatly valued as a packhorse for the Army, where their great strength was used to transport enormous loads. Purebreeding of the animals continued to develop in this organised fashion until 1914, when the outbreak of the First World War brought much more than just Haflinger breeding to a standstill. Most Haflingers were then requisitioned by the Army, mainly for use as pack animals to carry the great loads of equipment which could not be transported in any other way over the mountainous territory. With no one to enforce them, the breeding regulations soon ceased to be strictly adhered to, if at all, and the embryo Haflinger Breeders Co-operative was disbanded, leaving no body to oversee or offer guidance on breeding or to ensure continuation of the selective breeding progamme. The breed was about to face its first crisis. These were anxious days for the future of the Haflinger, and could have signalled the end of the purebred pony almost before it had become firmly established. The purebred pony might not have survived as we know it today, had there not been North Tyrolean breeders willing and able to build up their studs again, and with the knowledge and experience to trace the right type of breeding stock after the end of the war.

3 Development from 1918 to the present day

Several things happened very quickly after the end of the First World War. Perhaps the most significant as far as the Haflinger was concerned was the signing of the Treaty of St Germain, because this handed the South Tyrol over to Italy, whilst the North Tyrol remained as Austrian territory. The most serious problem to the future of Haflinger breeding was caused by the fact that most of the government-owned stallions (which was effectively almost all the Haflinger stallions) had been kept at the National Stallion Depot at Stadl-Paura in Upper Austria and most of the Haflinger brood mares had been kept in the South Tyrol where they remained. The mares and stallions thus became geographically separated and were now owned by people in different countries, and in some cases by different states.

Although attempts were made to resume the selective breeding programme in the South Tyrol quickly, and also to enlist the co-operation of the Italian government, these measures were not overly successful. To begin with, there was a great deal of animosity between the Austrians and the Italians as a result of the division of the Tyrol. The South Tyrolean Haflinger Breeders Co-operative were extremely unenthusiastic about working with Austrian breeders in the North Tyrol. The South Tyroleans pressed the Italian government for state approval and support and recommended that the few stallions remaining in South Tyrol should be subsidised, that every effort should be made to discourage crossbreeding between Haflingers and the other native Tyrolean breed, the Norican, and to continue to sponsor competitions as an inducement for breeders to retain high standards. Although some of these requests were met, the results were varied. In Genesio (Jenesien) some excellent quality animals were produced, as opposed to those from the nearby Sarentina (Sarn) Valley area where a great deal of crossbreeding had been in evidence even before the First World War, which had already led to many of the desirable Haflinger characteristics being lost in that area.

By 1921 the shortage of stallions in the South Tyrol was causing acute problems. The Italian government had introduced a number of stallions with Oriental blood, with the intention of improving the quality of the breeding stock, but in fact this measure did not prove to be a success. None of these bloodlines remains today. At the same time strenuous efforts were being made to increase the numbers as quickly as possible, which meant that many of the earlier strict standards were ignored, thus leading to a general decline in the quality of the breed in this region.

It was therefore left to the Austrians of the North Tyrol to somehow rescue the

Haflinger from a descent into obscurity almost before the modern breed had become properly established. At this time the breed was still not strong enough to hold its own amongst other old-established breeds in Austria without some fairly dedicated help. The private studs which had been breeding Haflingers before war broke out were not in a position to do very much as individuals, and if the majority of the stallions had not remained in Austria it is doubtful whether the pure breed would have survived. Even so, with the shortage of mares and the Austrian government's not surprising preoccupation with many matters it considered more important than Haflingers at this time, re-establishing a selective breeding programme was not easy.

In 1919 Rudolf Kohler, who was then the Austrian National Equine Breeding Supervisor, was given the task of redistributing the stallions from Stadl-Paura

throughout Austria in order to re-establish breeding across the country, despite there being very few good mares available. Five stallions were allowed to remain at Stadl-Paura and the rest were sent to studs which had been established before the war. Three stallions arrived in the North Tyrol, which was to become the leading area in the Austrian redevelopment of the breed – not unexpectedly, since the region was very similar in all ways to the Haflinger's original homeland in the South Tyrol. Two men had considerable influence on the development of the Haflinger at this time. Hermann Haueis of Zams in the west of the area and Andreas Thaler from Wildschonau were successive Ministers of Agriculture who had both been born and bred in the farming areas of the Tyrol, and they were quick to realise that Haflinger breeding could become an excellent source of additional income for the farmers of the region.

Haueis was a hotelier, who through the wine trade had many business contacts with the South Tyrol, which was how he had first become aware of the existence of the Haflinger. He proceeded to establish several studs in the Zams area and gradual-'ly as more people became interested, Haflinger breeding was soon under way in earnest in the North Tyrol. In 1921 the first North Tyrolean horse breeders co-operative with its headquarters in Zams was formed with Hermann Haueis as its chairman. It was known as the Zams Haflinger Breeders Co-operative. The following year saw the first Haflinger breed show at Zams. Rudolf Kohler was among a number of prominent personalities who attended that show.

In 1922 the stud of Huzulen horses, which had been established at Waldhof in Lower Austria, was disbanded. The mares were re-distributed to Haflinger breeders throughout Austria in an attempt to ease the general shortage of mares available for breeding. However, any hopes of producing quality Haflingers in this way appear to have been rapidly dashed as the Huzulen mares proved totally unsuitable for the North Tyrol, where the horses had to be able to work as well as to breed. In fact, these mares were not even good quality stock, and it was not long before it became clear that urgent efforts were needed to acquire some of the original Haflinger brood mares from the South Tyrol. Under the guidance of Hermann Haueis, the Breeders Co-operative initiated a policy of regular and continuous imports of South Tyrolean Haflinger mares. Initially it proved very difficult to get mares out of the South Tyrol, with most of the early consignments having to be smuggled across the border. However, later on, when the Austrian and Italian governments were on better terms with each other, the mares were imported legitimately.

In 1926 the North Tyrolean Breeders Co-operative compiled their first stud book for mares. Only purebred Haflinger mares which met the standards laid down by the

Co-operative were accepted for entry. Fortunately by this time a considerable number of mares had been acquired which did not meet these standards, so there was a good base of foundation stock available.

Two further Co-operatives were then formed in quick succession: the Weer Haflinger Breeders in 1927 and the Wildschonau Breeders in 1928. The Austrian Ministry of Agriculture approached the government of the South Tyrol in the late 1920s and negotiated an agreement to purchase one hundred of their good quality purebred Haflinger mares. The North Tyrol received seventy of these and the remainder were distributed in Upper Austria and Styria. Only the best quality mares had been selected and these, together with the quality stallions which were already established in Austria, formed an excellent basic foundation for further development of the breed.

The important task of continuing to ensure that control over the breeding of Haflingers throughout Austria was maintained was taken over in 1935 by Dr Karl Thurner. It was Dr Thurner who had been responsible for the first stud book in 1926 and he had later drawn up the first Haflinger stallion genealogical table.

The great depression which affected most of the world in the late 1920s and early 1930s also caused problems for Haflinger breeders, who found difficulty in selling their stock. However, by 1938 the equine market had revived considerably and suddenly Haflinger colts and crossbred foals which had previously been unsaleable were in great demand by the Army for pack animals. In fact, during the war years, Haflinger breeders received higher subsidies than they ever had before, or indeed have received since, for there was a regular and steady demand from the Army for the ponies. But even this brought difficulties, because the pressure to cover every Haflinger mare available meant that many unregistered mares were put in foal. This was in complete opposition to the principles of the strictly controlled breeding programme operated hitherto, and not surprisingly led to a decline in the quality. It was at this time also that the smaller Haflinger became more prevalent for a period. The early Haflingers had been bred to reach around 14.3 hh at maturity; now, however, mares being imported from the South Tyrol were only around 13.3 hh, and their foals tended to be smaller too. This smaller animal, which was also chunkier and stockier, became desirable during the war when Haflingers were in such great demand by the Army as pack horses. Although the policy changed again after the war to breed the taller, better quality ponies which are closer to the original Haflingers bred in the early years of the twentieth century, it took time for these changes to have visible effects. This has led to some differences of opinion in Haflinger breeding circles as to which is the more desirable type of animal.

Haflingers carrying equipment for the Austrian army on a training exercise in the Tyrol.

By the time the Second World War broke out, Haflinger breeding had become established in Bavaria in Germany, because the German Army had also discovered the advantages of Haflingers for pack work and rapidly developed an insatiable demand for them. Unfortunately, although the Bavarians started out with good quality stock (mainly from the South Tyrol), other inferior Haflingers and even some other breeds were introduced which actually led to a situation during the war when both crossbred mares and stallions were being registered. This situation arose because the Bavarian Purchasing Commission, which was responsible for choosing and registering the stock, were unable to keep up with the German Army's huge

16

demands for Haflingers and so less strict standards were maintained for registration. This led to inevitable problems for the Haflinger when purebreeding resumed in Bavaria after the war. Apart from Italy, which had of course become a Haflinger breeding country with the acquisition of the South Tyrol, Germany was the first European country (and the only other one prior to the Second World War) to see the potential in this versatile small horse.

There are a number of tales of Haflingers' feats of endurance during the war, but a particular escape from the impending Russian occupation in 1945 perhaps deserves to be recounted here. It is the story of a German family's return from Styria in Lower Austria, where they had established a small Haflinger stud, through occupied Austria and Germany to their native Westphalia.

The party consisted of three Haflingers and nine people. Two of the mares were harnessed to a wagon while the third, an unbroken three-year-old filly, was tied alongside. The family, comprising the grandmother, four younger women and four children (the youngest of which was a five-week-old baby), were all packed into the wagon, together with their essential luggage.

They left the farm just hours before the Russians moved in, and set off to beat the Russian Army's advance. For this first stage of the journey the Haflingers remained in harness for thirty-two hours without a break and with a minimum of stops for food and water. They were caught up in the retreat of the German Army; everyone was racing for the Enns river which was to become the border between the American and Russian zones. When the river was finally reached, it seemed initially that the Haflinger party would not be able to make the crossing in time as their brake cable had broken earlier and there was still a steep descent to make to the bridge. However, with a little help from friendly soldiers, temporary repairs were carried out and they crossed the river just one hour before the Russians took control of the zone.

This was by no means the end of the journey though. Because the family were German and they had no papers, it was still necessary to avoid the Americans and they had to keep away from the main routes, which meant difficult and mountainous territory to negotiate. Two additional horses were purchased at this stage to help the Haflingers by converting the team to a four-in-hand. The river Inn was the next destination to be reached, and this part of the journey took two weeks. After the Inn had been crossed the country became flatter so that the two extra horses were exchanged for food. A few days' break was also taken to enable more permanent repairs to be carried out on the wagon's brakes.

Once again the only horse power left was the Haflingers. At this point, despite the fact that she was unbroken, the three year old had to pull her weight – literally. She was put into harness, which she accepted without complaint, and the three Haflingers were from then on driven as a troika, a real demonstration of the Haflinger's willing and adaptable nature.

The journey continued, and even if the danger was not as great as in the beginning, it was certainly still fraught with hardships. When Westphalia was finally reached, 700 miles had been covered in just forty-nine days.

To end the tale, these three Haflingers became the foundation mares for the first Haflinger stud in Westphalia and continued to foal regularly for a number of years, despite the great strain put on them by this marathon journey.

The end of the Second World War was once again a critical time for the Haflinger. The Army no longer needed them as pack horses, their size had decreased and the Austrian government again had many more important matters on its mind than Haflinger breeding. Fortunately, however, the members of the Zams Haflinger Breeders Co-operative, which at this time became the Haflinger Breeders' Association of the Tyrol, were made of sterner stuff. They had already met in the summer of 1945 to lay plans for the future of the breed.

A number of decisions were made at that meeting, the most important being the necessity to return quickly to the strict breeding regulations which had applied up until 1938, in order to ensure that only good quality stock was bred from in the future. The stud book was reorganised: since 1946, the breed has been managed in mare families, which are formed by several generations of consistently good quality animals which frequently become the mothers of stallions. The man who was nominated to succeed Dr Thurner as the National Breeding Supervisor was Herr Otto Schweisgut. He made Haflinger breeding his life's work and remained Managing Director of the Haflinger Breeders' Association of the Tyrol for forty years, from 1945 to 1985, when he was succeeded by his son Johannes, known to all as Hannes. He was also managing Director of the Federation of Austrian Haflinger Breeders for twenty years, from 1965 to 1985.

In the years immediately following the war, the Tyrol was placed under American administration; the military Haflinger breeding centre at Zams, run by the Tyrolean Haflinger Breeders' Association, was therefore taken over by the Americans. There were around one hundred Haflinger stallions there at that time, but Otto Schweisgut was only allowed to retain thirty to begin his new programme of breeding. Sadly the remainder were slaughtered for meat, such were the shortages in those early postwar years.

Unfortunately a further setback occurred shortly after this when these surviving young stallions were turned out on the High Pasture in the Vorarlberg region, which

Hannes Schweisgut presents the trophy for the best novice mare to Helen Robbins' Silverton Ottilia, watched by Otto Schweisgut at the British Breed Show 1991.

was then occupied by French forces. One day the stallions mysteriously went missing. Rumours circulated of them having been seen being loaded on to a train, but they had disappeared without any further trace. Despite the strenuous efforts which were made to find them (which included appeals to the French government at the highest levels), they were never seen again.

In spite of this unfortunate incident, the stallion stock was eventually replenished by bringing the younger colts on as potential stallions. However, the programme was delayed for a period and some good stock was sadly lost for ever.

Herr Schweisgut faced an uphill task. In order to re-establish the Haflinger as quickly as possible he made two important changes to earlier policy. First of all the various Haflinger Breeders' Associations of the Tyrol were amalgamated into a single organisation which in turn created one central stud (now the *Fohlenhof* at Ebbs) run by this organisation, and secondly the control of all stallions acquired by the stud and of which mares those stallions should be mated with, was all vested in Herr Schweisgut himself as Director of Breeding (Managing Director) of the Haflinger Breeders' Association of the Tyrol, which was a government appointment. His policy has always been to retain absolute purity of the breed. By accepting Herr Schweisgut's policy and giving him full control of the entire Tyrolean breeding programme, the Association had demonstrated its enormous trust in his knowledge, ability and integrity to further the best interests of the Haflinger breed.

The stud which the Schweisguts manage at Ebbs, near Kufstein on the Austrian–German border, in addition to producing quality stock is the main sales and training centre for Haflingers in the Tyrol. The annual sales are attended by breeders and enthusiasts from all over the world. The stud is run nowadays by Hannes, although Herr Schweisgut senior still takes a very keen interest in all the proceedings.

Contrary to some expectations there was a demand for the breed even in the early postwar years. Many areas lacked horses altogether, so farmers unable to obtain heavier horses for their farm requirements found themselves having to use a Haflinger. The farmers soon found out that this was no real hardship, as the Haflingers were just as capable of carrying out all the work required of them as their heavier cousins were. Their great strength in relation to their size, their surefootedness on the steep mountain slopes and their sound constitutions all compared very favourably with the larger breeds.

By 1947 the policy of pure breeding had been introduced to the whole of the Tyrol and the Haflinger Breeders' Association of the Tyrol had established its own stallion centre at Ebbs. As a result of this government policy, all Tyrolean stallions then became the property of the Tyrolean State; no private individual in the Tyrol was permitted to keep a stallion. This meant that total control of the stallions, and therefore of the male breeding lines, was maintained by Herr Schweisgut in his capacity as Managing Director of the Haflinger Breeders' Association. However, in other areas of Austria the rules were different and a few stallions did remain in private ownership. The prefix 'liz.' indicates those stallions which are not the property of the state: 'liz.' is short for *lizenz* which translated means 'licence', or in this context 'permitted' (to be privately owned). Today, with State funds becoming ever more tightly stretched, as indeed they are everywhere in Europe, more stallions are reverting to private ownership and now it is even permitted in the Tyrol. Of the fourteen three-year-old colts which were passed as stallions at the 1993 inspections at Ebbs, all were designated 'liz.'.

However, in 1947, because three years' worth of stallion stock had been lost following the unfortunate disappearance of the thirty young stallions from Zams, the Tyrolean breeders had to make attempts to obtain animals born during those three years from the South Tyrol. Not very surprisingly, the South Tyroleans were unwilling to sell any high quality young stallions so the Austrians were forced to look to the older stallions in order to replenish their breeding stock. Thus Anselmo was purchased from Italy at the age of twenty, along with a couple of other older animals.

By 1950 the Tyrolean breeding programme was well under way. Over the next twenty-four years, the number of registered brood mares increased from 1562 to 2043 despite the fact that the equine population in the world had dropped from some 16.5 million to around 6.5 million. However, the Austrians left nothing to chance; they had realised very early on that it would be necessary to spend time and money promoting the Haflinger as a versatile and marketable commodity, sought after not only in Austria but throughout Europe and, eventually, the world. This turned out to be a wise move, because the Norwegian Fjord horse had also arrived in Germany in the 1950s and was soon offering strong competition for the Haflinger, both there and in other European countries.

Throughout the 1950s and 1960s Haflinger breeding policy in the Tyrol set the standards for the breed elsewhere. Quality control was strict and only the very best stock was permitted to be used for breeding.

In 1951 a horse show was held at Zams to which Haflinger breeders from Italy, Germany and Austria were invited, together with Swiss breeders who had shown an interest in the Haflinger. At this meeting objectives for the future of Haflinger breeding were worked out by these countries. However, despite this beginning, it was not until 1976 that the World Haflinger Federation was formed.

During the 1950s Haflingers became established in what was West Germany, Switzerland and Yugoslavia as well as continuing to thrive in Italy. In 1956 Haflingers arrived in the former East Germany and in 1958 the first Haflingers were exported to Illinois in the USA. Czechoslovakia had entered the market in 1959 when they purchased Haflinger stallions, initially for crossbreeding with Huzulen mares in an attempt to improve that breed.

In 1961 the Tyrolean Haflinger Breeders' Association organised a major show in Innsbruck where the concept of mare families was introduced to the general equestrian public, in order to emphasise the importance of the female line. A number of

A Haflinger family group exhibited at the *Fohlenhof.*

mares ranging in age from twenty to thirty years, each having delivered at least ten foals, were exhibited as families. Each family had to represent at least four generations. Ten stallion groups were also exhibited, with each stallion having sired at least ten daughters. Family groups are now an integral part of the World Haflinger Show. The first international Haflinger stallion genealogical table was also published at this show. The table included all registered stallions of those nations breeding Haflingers at that time.

Also in 1961, Holland and Turkey purchased Haflingers for the first time. By 1963 there were thirteen nations recorded as being Haflinger breeders. The growth of the breed continued throughout the 1960s with France, Belgium, Poland, Hungary, Albania and Great Britain joining the ranks. In 1968 the first Haflingers were exported to Bhutan in the Himalayas, which then encouraged people in other parts of Asia to become interested in the breed.

The first International Haflinger Show was held in 1965 at Innsbruck. Every country which had become a Haflinger breeding nation was invited, but only Italy, Germany, Holland and Switzerland actually attended, in addition of course to the Austrians. Since then the World Haflinger Show has grown enormously and now has

22

an intercontinental attendance far beyond the dreams of those early days. The show is now held every five years.

The 1970s saw the Haflinger continue to flourish and become established in many more new countries, including Luxembourg, Denmark, Sweden, Ireland, Thailand, Canada, Australia, Columbia, Brazil and Namibia (South West Africa). By the end of the 1970s the Haflinger could be found on every continent. The driving force behind this incredible worldwide promotion was of course the Tyrolean Haflinger Breeders' Association, and in particular Herr Otto Schweisgut. If one had to name just one person who has had the greatest influence on Haflinger breeding and promotion, it is undoubtedly Herr Schweisgut. For more than forty years his life has been dedicated to the Haflinger.

The Italian stallion Hafling, sired by Nautilus and born in 1952, at the first International Haflinger Show held at Innsbruck in 1965.

In 1976 the World Haflinger Federation was formed to unite national Haflinger breeders associations with the aim of promoting, improving and increasing the population of purebred Haflingers worldwide. Herr Otto Schweisgut was elected the first president. Dr Willi Krapf of Switzerland, M. Leon LePetit of France and Mrs Mary Bromily of Great Britain were invited to be the first three vice presidents. The British Society's chairman, Tom Crane, is one of the current vice presidents, having been appointed on the resignation of Mary Bromily. Inge Nobel of Denmark and R. W. McArthur of the USA have also been appointed more recently as vice presidents.

National Haflinger associations are only permitted to become members of the World Haflinger Federation if they agree to promote purebreeding and follow the principles of the Federation to ensure that the hereditary characteristics of the breed are retained. They are also required to maintain a stud book for purebred Haflingers, and separate partbred stud books must be kept for those animals which have Arabian or other blood.

Haflinger breeding has continued throughout the world during the 1980s and into the 1990s, with numbers increasing all the time. Where the country is a member of the World Haflinger Federation, the policy developed by the Austrians is closely followed, since the rules drawn up by the World Haflinger Federation are based on that policy.

The Haflinger is a most adaptable animal and although the breed originated in a northern hemisphere Alpine environment, the very fact that these ponies are now bred worldwide without the essential characteristics of the breed changing demonstrates admirably their adaptability. As mentioned earlier, young Haflingers in Austria are expected to spend their summers on the *Alms* where they experience considerable ranges of temperature and differences in altitude. This may be a contributory factor to their ability to survive widely differing environments, from the intense dry heat of Australia to the humid heat of India and the extreme cold of the winters in Canada. They have even been known to withstand Arctic winters where temperatures fall to as low as -50 °C.

The Austrians will no doubt continue to lead the development of the breed into the twenty-first century, while the opening up of the European continent as a result of the fall of the Iron Curtain combined with the development of the European Union should see the Haflinger fully accepted alongside the other member countries' own native breeds.

Breeding and bloodlines

The general development of the Haflinger over the last 120 years has been considered in the previous chapters. Like any breed it has evolved with changing objectives, and while the principles remain the same, some changes have naturally taken place during this period.

At the beginning of the twentieth century the Haflinger was being used as a draught and pack horse in the mountains. The requirements for this job and the working conditions had to be taken into consideration in the early days of selective breeding. A broad back and chest, deep girth, short cannon bones and good paces, combined with agility and surefootedness was needed to work in mountainous territory. The early Haflingers had short muscular necks with broad short heads, and were taller than today, measuring up to 15 hh.

Some forty years later the breed was smaller, possibly as a result of limited breeding opportunities during the two world wars, despite the efforts made during the 1930s to improve the animals. By 1946, some stood less than 13 hh, at the lower end of the scale, rising to a maximum of about 14.2 hh. Additionally, by this time the Haflinger was being used as a riding animal and although the broad back and chest and deep girth were still very much in evidence, the neck and the back had become longer and the shoulder improved to give a better length of stride, so that it was just as suitable under saddle as it was for driving purposes or for use as a packhorse. The short broad head with the slightly 'dished' appearance, no doubt attributable to the Arabian ancestry, has changed little from the very early Haflingers right up to the present day. As well as the previously mentioned improvements to the stride, the modern policy is once again to breed taller animals, by using only the taller mares and stallions for breeding, because of their increasing popularity amongst adults for ridden activities. Ponies under 14 hh are less marketable as a ride for adults.

The Haflinger is now bred in Austria as an all-round horse, mainly for pleasure, although there are still some working the farms. It must be reliable, willing and surefooted whether under saddle or in harness. Over the last fifty years the temperament has also featured as an important consideration in selection for breeding. While Haflingers have always been known for their kind and quiet nature, this has been one of the official standards taken into consideration by breeders and inspectors since the Schweisguts assumed prominence in the Tyrolean breeding programme.

The Haflinger should of course meet the general standards of good conformation.

Austrian harness is heavy but the Haflinger carries it well.

Such defects as sickle hocks, pigeon toes, ewe neck, parrot jaw and so on are as
unacceptable in a Haflinger as in any breed.

The overall picture should be a pleasing one. Starting with the head, there should
be a clear and expressive eye, clean slender jowls and a fine poll. The head should be
well set on a neck of reasonable length leading to a long and sloping shoulder. There

should be good breadth of chest. The withers need to be sufficiently pronounced to ensure that the saddle can be placed in the correct position without any marked tendency to slip forward. The girth should be deep, and the back a good length without being too long, but it should not present a dipped appearance. The limbs should be clean, strong and have good bone substance with broad flat knees and wide powerful hocks. The tail is set slightly lower than in some breeds but should not be set too deep. The hooves are normally hard and round with well developed pasterns. That is the description of an ideal Haflinger, and while no horse is perfect and some minor faults are acceptable, any serious deviation from the ideal standard means that that animal should not be used for breeding purposes.

In order to ensure that these high standards are met and only good quality stock is used for breeding, the Austrians have evolved a strict system of inspection. The Tyrolean Haflinger Breeders Association is also committed to conscientious maintenance of the stud book, which is essential if the inspection system is to remain valid. No mares are permitted to be covered before they have been inspected and accepted into the stud book. After a mare has been covered there is a set procedure to be followed. A covering certificate showing the pedigrees of both sire and dam is issued at the time of service and must be signed by the stallion director. The reverse of this certificate is then completed on the birth of the foal. Foals are inspected within six months of birth and while long-term development cannot be accurately assessed at this age, those considered to have stallion or brood mare potential are branded and given their own pedigree certificate. At three years old the youngsters are all inspected again, this time against the pre-determined standards. Mares passed are placed in one of ten categories before being entered into the main stud book. These mares are finally branded with the Eidelweiss on the left flank to show they have passed inspection and been accepted into the stud book.

The Eidelweiss brand which marks mares and stallions who have passed inspection.

27

Inspection is based on a 100-point system whereby a minimum of 5 points and a maximum of 10 points are awarded in ten different categories. Attention is given to height, conformation, bone and action. A final overall quality assessment follows which includes consideration of the temperament and colour. White markings are acceptable on the face only and there should be no grey- or chestnut-coloured hair in the mane or tail, which should be white or flaxen, where this gives a gold or silver sheen without the presence of other coloured hair (Haflingers are not palominos, and albinos are not produced). Any animal which receives less than 60 points at inspection or less than 5 out of 10 for the overall quality assessment will not be accepted in the stud book.

The ten areas assessed are: Type, Head, Neck, Forehand, Mid-body, Hindquarters, Front Limbs, Hind Limbs, Correctness of Gait and Length of Stride.

The overall classification according to points scored is as follows:

Points Awarded	Class
85 or more	Ib+
83 to 84	Ib
81 to 82	Ib–
79 to 80	IIa+
77 to 78	IIa
75 to 76	IIa–
73 to 74	IIb+
71 to 72	IIb
66 to 70	IIb–
60 to 65	III

Only mares whose pedigree is fully registered as purebred for six generations are even considered for acceptance into the stud book and minimum height standards also have to be met when determining which class a mare is assigned to.

There is a separate stallion register and very high standards indeed have to be met before a stallion is accepted into the register. Colts may not even be considered for stallions unless their dam's pedigree is impeccable. Stallions, as well as having to meet the set height and other standards in the same way as the mares, are also assessed on likely breeding strength (which is the degree to which a stallion passes on his desirable traits) and hereditary reliability. The stallion's registration certificate also shows a pedigree going back four generations, and a record of mares covered,

numbers and sexes of foals born, and the percentage of aborted pregnancies, still births and live births from mares covered. All this information is made use of when deciding which stallions are suitable for covering which mares. Stallions accepted into the stud book are branded with the Eidelweiss on the left flank in the same way as the mares.

Out of all the colts born in the Tyrol each year, only between sixty and one hundred are selected at the initial inspection as potential breeding stallions. The best fifty of these are then sent to the *Fohlenhof* at Ebbs which is the main Tyrolean Stallion Centre, in order that the best twenty-five or so may be selected for specialised stallion raising. The breeders of all those colts not selected are required either to geld them or to sell them outside the Tyrolean breeding region. The Breeders' Association undertakes to obtain the best possible price it can for such animals as compensation for the breeder. The selected colts are then measured at approximately six-monthly intervals until the young stallions reach the age of three, when they are fully inspected again and the Director of the Tyrolean Breeders' Association selects those he considers the most suitable to retain for the Tyrolean breeding region. These stallions are then purchased from the Association by the Austrian Ministry of Agriculture and made available for use throughout the region. The others which have passed as stallions may be sold elsewhere or exported. As a point of interest, some 95 per cent of all Haflinger stallions used for breeding throughout Austria have come from the Tyrolean Centre at Ebbs. All animals not passed as stallions at the final inspections must be gelded, although in practice geldings are not held in any esteem in Austria and are fortunate if they end up as working animals. Many in fact go to the meat market, although the better quality gelding are slowly beginning to be accepted for riding or driving purposes.

Stallion raising in the Tyrol is strictly controlled. It must be remembered that unlike this country, in the Tyrol and in much of the rest of Austria, stallions are mainly state owned and therefore most individuals who breed colt foals have no say in how the foal will be reared if it is considered to be potential stallion material. All colts in the Tyrol destined to become stallions are raised at the *Fohlenhof*, where they are kept as a herd to encourage play, which helps build up the muscles and also teaches the youngsters to develop their courage by defending themselves in playful combat. They are kept within their own age groups and during the winter months live in barn type stabling, although they do spend several hours out of doors each day. In about May they are taken up to the lower *Alms* which are at an altitude of around 3600 feet (1100 m). From July to September they spend their time on the high *Alms* where the altitude is some 5600 feet (1700 m). They go back to the lower *Alms* in mid-September, where they remain until November when they return to the *Fohlenhof* for the winter.

In Haflinger breeding, although the mare lines are of great importance, it is the stallion lineage to which all Haflingers are referred. There are seven stallion bloodlines and each is named from the first letter of the founding stallion's name. All stallion lines can be traced back to the founding stallion Folie. Except in Italy, where each year the youngsters are given a name beginning with a pre-determined alpha character, the names of all Haflinger colts begin with the first character of their sire's name and the fillies are named using the first letter of their dam's name. Generally speaking this makes it simple to identify a stallion's line, although the Italians have caused some confusion by using a different system. The mare lines are a little more complicated to follow.

The modern A-line was founded by Anselmo, a great great great grandson of Folie born in 1926, whose ancestry traces back via the early foundation stallion Campi. The B-line founder was Bolzano, born in 1915, who was a great great grandson of Folie. Massimo, a great great great grandson of Folie born in 1927, founded the M-line. The N-line was founded by Nibbio, born in 1920, another great great great grandson of Folie, as was Stelvio, founder of the S-line foaled in 1923, and Student, founder of the ST-line foaled in 1927. These last five lines all trace back to

Folie via two of the early foundation stallions, his grandson Genter and Genter's son liz. Mandl. Finally, the W-line, founded by liz. Willi, a great great grandson of Folie, can be traced back via the early foundation stallions, Jenner and liz. Hafling.

Today the A-line is considered to be one of the strongest, with the second largest number of stallions at stud. It is also considered to combine well with all the other lines. However, in the late 1940s there was concern that it might not survive due to the lack of quality stallions available in the early postwar years. The purchase by the Tyroleans of Anselmo himself at the age of twenty-one was a somewhat desperate attempt at saving the line which ultimately justified itself. Although Anselmo was a somewhat coarse stallion he had already produced a number of good mares. At the time of purchase, however, he had not yet proved himself as a sire of stallions. His

Anselmo, born in 1926 and sired by Campi II out of Napoli, founder of the modern A-line.

liz. Afghan, born in 1969 and sired by Artist out of Jaruse, was an outstanding Haflinger stallion.

31

age made it necessary to initiate a speedy programme of breeding, particularly in the hope of producing suitable stallion stock. He stood at stud for seven years and during that time produced four quality stallions, Atlas, Alex, Attila and Adler, of which the latter was considered to be the best. The A-line was strengthened substantially through Adler and is now represented in all the Haflinger breeding countries in the world. In Austria today the progeny of liz. Afghan (son of Artist who was a grandson of Adler) tends to dominate the A-line.

The B-line was not present at all in the North Tyrol when the Tyrolean Breeders Association began the serious business of establishing all the Haflinger lines firmly in the region, so it was a difficult task both to establish and build up a strong B-line in this area. In due course, however, a young B-line stallion named Bozen was purchased from the South Tyrol where this line is strongest, and established in the North Tyrol. He produced the stallion Brenner whose offspring led to a solid B-line in Austria, although elsewhere this line is either weak or non-existent. Brutus, a grandson of Brenner born in 1976, is considered to be an excellent quality stallion through which the B-line is stabilising. He was sold by the Austrians to Germany, where he

Brutus, born in 1976 and sired by Becket out of a mare from the Beatrix-Penzl strain, is considered to be the first Austrian quality B-line stallion.

has produced a number of stallions which are now spread over several European countries. His first son, Benjo, sired Bergwind who is now one of the key B-line stallions in Austria. Another of his sons, Bernhard, came to Great Britain and sired Clifton Brunel who was exported to the USA.

The Italian stallion Massimo, who was founder of the modern M-line, sired six sons, of which Nilo was the most significant in continuing the line. He carried excellent bloodlines both from his sire and also from his dam, who carried quality blood

Mordskerl, born in 1938 and sired by Nilo, had significant influence on the Austrian M-line.

from the stallions Nibbio and Mölten. The former was of particular significance since Mölten's line has died out today. Three of Nilo's sons are regarded as being important, but liz. Stürmer (not to be confused with the ST-line stallion of the same name), purchased by the Austrians, was probably the most significant. He produced a strong male line and also high quality daughters who were used to strengthen the A-line. His sons Marius, Midas and Magnat were the best of his male progeny and ensured the continuation of the M-line in Austria, together with offspring of Mordskerl, who was another of Nilo's sons to have a significant influence on the continuation of the line. The third son of Nilo, Meteor, remained in Italy to continue the Italian M-line.

The N-line developed into two branches very early on. The founding stallion, Nibbio, belonged to Italy and the main Austrian N-line developed through liz. Naz, a grandson of Nibbio, while the Italian N-line continued through Ilio and his son

liz. Naz, born in 1941 and sired by the Italian stallion Bacco, ensured the development of the main Austrian N-line.

Nautilus. The N-line is a very strong stallion line, with the greatest number of stallions at stud. It is the only other one (together with the A-line) which is represented in every Haflinger breeding country. The N-line is currently most prolific in Italy and Germany. In Austria the N-line is flourishing through the progeny of Norden, whose ancestry can be traced directly back to liz. Naz.

The S-line, founded by the stallion Stelvio, is considered to be the weakest of all the stallion lines. Austria acquired Stelvio's great great grandson, the stallion Salurn, from Italy in the mid 1960s in the hope of building up the strength of this line. Salurn produced three stallions and his first son, Silber, produced three more, the best of which was Silbersee. This stallion went to Germany and because non-Haflinger blood was introduced, the Silbersee line is now threatened with extinction. The Austrians are endeavouring to continue their S-line through Saturn, whose grandson

Silbersee, born in 1972 and sired by Silber. His line seems unlikely to continue.

Salut has produced some quality offspring. Two new S-line stallions, one sired by Salut and one by a Salut son, were registered in 1992. Currently the S-line is strongest in Italy.

The ST-line today has a large number of stallions but because of less than careful and selective breeding in some countries where it has virtually disappeared, it is not found spread over as wide a geographical area as might be expected. Student was the founder, and two of his sons in the Tyrol, Stromer and Aldrian, ensured a sound base for the line through their sons. Stromer was the more prolific of the the two, producing Steiger, Stolz, Stüber, Sturmwind, Strom and Stern. The Stüber line, particularly through his great grandson Stürmer, influenced the Austrian ST breeding considerably, despite the fact that Stürmer died young at the age of only eight years.

Stüber, born in 1957 and sired by Stromer, had considerable influence on the Austrian ST-line through his great grandson Stürmer.

Steinadler, born in 1965 and sired by Stüber, has produced a strong branch of the ST-line.

Fortunately a number of his sons remain to continue the line. The Steinadler branch of this line is also producing quality stallions. Outside Austria there are strong branches of the ST-line in the former East Germany and in the USA.

Although the founding stallion of the W-line, liz. Willi, produced many stallions, the two which produced the best lines were Willi I and Wardein. Willi I's son Wilfried went to Bavaria where he sired Wieland, a seemingly excellent stallion which initially gave great hope for a strong W-line. However, in the second generation his stock suddenly began to deteriorate and by the third generation had died out. It was later discovered that the reason for this was the fact that Wieland's dam had not possessed a pedigree and undesirable traits apparently lay dormant, only to surface in later generations. There were other sons of Willi I who produced continuing

liz. Willi, born in 1921 and sired by Sarn, was the founder of the W-line.

Wardein, born in 1938 and sired by liz. Willi, consolidated the Austrian W-line.

lines but these were mainly in Holland, Canada and the USA. Fortunately for the future of the W-line in the Tyrol there was still Wardein. His pedigree was impeccable and even in his twenties he still sired several good stallions. Two of them, Wirbel and Wilten, remained in Austria and consolidated the W-line there, while a third, Winchester, was exported to the former East Germany where he founded a strong W-line. The Italian W-line traces back to Wilten. Wildmoos, a grandson of Wirbel, probably has the most significant influence on the Austrian W-line today. This line is also well established in the USA and Holland.

In order to try and ensure that the most desirable characteristics and traits are passed on, the Austrians ensured from an early stage that the best possible mares were mated selectively with specific stallions. A certain amount of in-breeding has also been carried out (albeit carefully) in an attempt to concentrate the particularly desirable characteristics. It was this process which was used to strengthen the A-line as rapidly as possible without producing large numbers of inferior animals.

When selecting suitable animals for mating, Herr Schweisgut's policy was that the individual characteristics of the mare and stallion should be balanced against one another. However, even this is not totally foolproof and it is known that two full brothers or two full sisters can pass on quite different traits. Despite the fact that they have identical parentage, they have inherited different genes. This is where the luck factor comes in. The major concern is whether or not an animal can pass on undesirable traits and this is more difficult to predict, since not all defects are dominant or even appear in the next generation – it is quite possible to miss a generation as happened in the case of the W-line stallion Wieland. Likewise, invisible traits such as poor temperament are not always apparent in the youngster but may only develop with age, by which time the mare or stallion may already have passed the defect on. In the end, however scientific one tries to be in selecting animals for breeding, the result comes only from a certain amount of expertise combined with instinct and an element of luck.

Although in-breeding can increase the possibility of producing poor stock, used carefully it can also magnify the desirable characteristics. The Haflinger's kind and willing temperament, its adaptability and simple dietary requirements are all traits which have been very important since the days when most Haflingers were owned by poor mountain farmers who could not afford more than one horse. The Haflinger therefore had to fulfil all the needs of its owner including being economical to keep. If all these needs could not be met, the animal was of no use.

In the late 1800s when the modern Haflinger's development first began, where an animal exhibited all the required characteristics, the farmers practised in-breeding without being aware of the scientific aspects, because they knew it gained the desired end result of producing the best possible animal to suit their needs. Animals not meeting the required standards were discarded since they were of no use on the farm. Therefore, although by instinct more than science, the 'selective' breeding practised by the early farmer breeders led to excellent quality stock on which to build the pure Haflinger breed when a more scientific approach was later taken.

In Austria crossbreeding is frowned upon. Herr Schweisgut is of the opinion that there are plenty of suitable riding pony or driving pony types on the market, but the Haflinger has its own market where it meets the requirements of an all-round horse which can perform at all levels and in a wide variety of disciplines, both under saddle and in harness. He expresses concern about activities in some countries where breeding activities are producing what amount to Arab/Haflinger crossbreds. The

Germans in particular have introduced a great deal of Arab blood (up to 25 per cent) into some of their Haflinger bloodlines, which has resulted in the loss of some of the essential Haflinger characteristics from some of these lines. A case in point is the Silbersee line which is in danger of dying out as a result of this introduction of non-Haflinger blood. At one time these 'Haflinger–Arab' type animals were included in the main stud book in Westphalia, but now they have been separated. After six more generations they are permitted to be re-entered in the main stud book as pure Haflingers. This, however, is only applicable in Germany. Nevertheless, Herr Schweisgut admits that there are instances where using Haflingers on other breeds have produced improvements in that breed – for example, the introduction of Haflinger blood into the Huzulen horse of the former Czechoslovakia. However, the policy of the Haflinger Breeders' Association of the Tyrol remains firmly committed to purebreeding only in the Tyrolean region.

The decision in 1947 to make the commitment to purebreeding only brought certain problems. Its introduction required new laws to be passed in support of it, and to this end amendments had to be made to the Tyrolean Animal Husbandry Laws. At this time there were only two legally recognised breeds of horse in the Tyrol, the Haflinger and the Norican. Nowadays, however, Arabs, Austrian Standardbreds (Trotters) and other breeds of pony are also accepted and officially bred there.

Having committed themselves to this course of action, the Tyrolean Haflinger Breeders' Association then set about putting their policies into practice. In order to retain firm control over breeding, it was decided that all stallions should be state owned and therefore one of the first pieces of new legislation prohibited the private ownership of any stallion. Not surprisingly this produced problems of its own. Because Haflingers reach maturity at an early age and yearling colts are quite capable of covering yearling fillies, provision had to be made for separating the youngsters as soon as possible. This led to all the colts which were selected as potential stallions being sent to the *Fohlenhof* for raising by the Association. All other colts then had to be gelded if they were to be retained. Strict control also had to be exercised over all the studs to ensure that these regulations were being adhered to. In the past, before private ownership of stallions was made illegal, breeders in remote areas had not always used approved stallions due to the distance they would have had to travel their mares. A little judicious bribery could obtain a covering certificate without much difficulty. With the new rules in force, any studs not conforming were subject to certain exclusion from the approved breeders lists and faced possible expulsion from the Association. It is only recently that private ownership of stallions has been permitted again in the Tyrol.

Other problems also arose from a somewhat less expected fact: visually many Haflingers are difficult to distinguish between due to their uniformity of colour and similarity of markings. Even grooms who have worked regularly amongst the colts can find it hard to recognise some of them when they return to the *Fohlenhof* from the *Alms*. At the *Fohlenhof*, therefore, all colts are issued with a number which is shaved on to their quarters, a process which has to be repeated at regular intervals until the animal receives his final assessments for registration as a stallion, when it is branded permanently. Currently a new method of identification is being introduced, that of electronic tagging. This was pioneered by the American breeders and is not only an effective way of preventing confusion over the identity of youngsters, but also provides a permanent identification of the animal throughout its life.

It is undoubtedly the Austrians' determination to overcome these and many other obstacles which has led to the production of the quality animal which the purebred Haflinger has become today. Although there is probably a place for crossbreeding, in order to crossbreed successfully one must first have a pure breed with which to begin the process. Therefore the importance which the Austrians place on purebreeding should in no way be underestimated.

5 Care, competition and training

Haflingers thrive whether they are kept out of doors or inside. However, although they can withstand very low temperatures, they need shelter from the wind and rain in winter. In their native Austria those belonging to farmers are often kept in stalls underneath the farmhouse during the winter and are turned out for the summer. Where they are stabled, the accommodation should meet the standards required for any other equine: that is, well ventilated, draughtproof and of sufficient size to permit freedom of movement.

Haflingers are rarely satisfied with the grass on their side of the fence; that on the other side is usually much more interesting and ponies kept outside need strong fencing. Post and rails are excellent but must be high enough to prevent the pony from leaning over to reach the grass on the other side – which it assuredly will do if there is the smallest chance! The rails should be close enough together to keep the animal from putting his head between them, or alternatively, sheep wire can be fixed to the posts behind the rails for the same reason. It may also be necessary to add an electric wire along the top rail to prevent them rubbing their manes and tails which are so long and thick that they can get very hot. A field shelter or a thick hedge to provide protection from the prevailing wind is also essential.

The Haflinger is a good doer and there are far more problems caused by fat Haflingers than thin ones. Nevertheless, this does not mean that a Haflinger does not need to be fed! Hard feed, however, should be strictly related to the amount of work an animal is required to do and in general non-heating nuts are sufficient to meet this need. Additionally, in winter all Haflingers need between 18 and 22 pounds of hay per day. Foals, of course, require especially good feeding with extra protein during their first year. Of course, one must be aware of the dangers of overfeeding protein to foals, although Haflingers have never been known to contract epiphysitis. However, the occasional case of contracted tendons has occurred. Mineral licks and other supplements may also be given. In summer it may be necessary to restrict their grazing quite severely, particularly where the pasture is lush. In Austria when they are out on the *Alms*, the grazing is fairly sparse and quite a lot of energy is used up just searching for food. In Britain, summer grazing tends to be much richer, hence the need for restriction. It is very easy for a Haflinger to become overweight but much harder to get that weight off again. Not only is it bad for their health to be seriously overweight but it also makes saddle fitting difficult, which in turn often gives a much less pleasant and comfortable ride because the saddle will have a tendency to slip.

Haflingers, like other horses, also need regular grooming with extra attention required where their manes and tails are concerned. Haflingers' manes and tails are one of their most attractive features and should be carefully brushed and kept tangle free. They should be washed in good weather, to help keep them soft and silky. Manes and tails should *never* be pulled or trimmed, except for the very end of the tail which may be cut level when it becomes too long. Generally speaking, Haflingers have strong hooves and some can and do work unshod. Nevertheless, they still need care from the farrier every six weeks or so. Haflingers like humans but they do prefer a one-to-one relationship; for this reason it is better if they can be looked after by just one or two people. This may not always be easy in a large establishment but if an animal is being prepared for a special event or activity, it will be happier if the groom does not change too often.

Breaking and schooling young Haflingers is no different from training any other young equine and plenty of books have been written on that subject, so it is not pro-

The Haflinger is a good doer but care needs to be taken that it does not get too fat on rich pasture.

posed to go into the fundamentals of breaking and schooling a horse in this book. However, a common mistake made with Haflingers is to break them in when they are too young. Because a Haflinger tends to look adult at a reasonably early age it has frequently and erroneously been assumed that they also mature at an early age. It has even been suggested, sometimes by those who should know better, that they can be broken in and ridden as two year olds. This is not so. Two year olds are still very much babies and neither have they developed sufficient muscle or bone nor have their brains matured enough to cope with the amount of stress which would be imposed if they were expected to work at this early stage. In general, three years old is quite soon enough to commence formal training. However, this is not to say that a youngster should not be taught basic manners, to lead in hand and to become accustomed to having his feet attended to by the farrier. This type of early training is recommended because Haflingers, despite their gentle natures, are very strong and can become pushy if not checked from the beginning. Some long reining and lungeing at about two and a half years old does no harm either. As Haflingers are generally amenable and anxious to please, there are usually few problems when their serious training does commence, provided they have been firmly handled from the beginning.

In the Tyrol, the Austrians begin training the ponies at the age of two and a half by breaking them to harness. They believe that it is easier to teach a horse broken to drive subsequently to accept a rider, rather than the other way round. Additionally, at two and a half, they are still too young to be ridden. When the pony has become accustomed to pulling a carriage it then progresses to being broken and schooled for riding. In Great Britain, since many Haflingers are kept for both riding and driving, they are often broken to both harness and saddle as youngsters also, although this is not necessarily so nor always in that order.

Once broken and schooled, Haflingers are capable of participating in any sphere of equestrian activity. In Austria the *Fohlenhof* at Ebbs also runs a leading riding and driving training school. The Haflingers here regularly compete in jumping, dressage and driving events. Many of the horses at Ebbs have reached the elementary level in dressage and some have achieved medium and advanced levels. The stallion Stuart is especially successful in dressage and has performed with a rider who was trained by the Spanish Riding School in Vienna. The stallions liz. Afghan and Stürmer were particularly good jumpers and liz. Afghan was recorded as having cleared 5 foot 3 inches in 1975. Austrian Haflingers also compete very successfully in all combinations of driving from singles and tandems to up to eight-in-hand. Teams of Haflingers from Austria have competed in Britain at the Windsor Driving Trials.

At this point it is perhaps appropriate to take a closer look at the *Fohlenhof*. Just after the war, in 1947, part of the Wagrein Castle Estate was leased by the Tyrolean Haflinger Breeders' Association to set up their new stallion centre. In 1959 the Estate came up for sale and they were able to purchase it. From that time on the *Fohlenhof* steadily expanded. Today, as well as being the National Stallion Centre, it is also the largest Haflinger stud not only in Austria but in Europe. Since 1964, when the stallion centre at Piber was finally disbanded, the *Fohlenhof* has been Austria's only Haflinger stallion centre. During the 1970s, as interest in the Haflinger continued to grow, the Riding and Driving School was developed, including residential facilities for riders and drivers undertaking training courses. It is also open to the public and the visitor can see stallions from each of the bloodlines together with mare families of several generations. One can also watch riding lessons in the indoor school from the comfort of the restaurant. Regular demonstrations of riding, driving and vaulting are held, to show off the versatility of the modern Haflinger. A major event each autumn is the annual foal auction sale (the first of which was held in 1966) of colts and fillies, which attracts buyers from all over the world. British buyers attend regularly. These sales are highly organised; the animals' order in the catalogue and the sale running order are arranged in bloodlines. Each bloodline is then subdivided into groups depending on quality, with the best quality foals in each bloodline being offered for sale first. Prices are high – top quality animals fetch as much as £10,000 and even lesser quality ones fetch well in excess of £1,000. In 1994 £16,470, the highest price ever achieved for a Haflinger filly at auction, was paid for Maserata, bred by Werner Beck. Rightly, the *Fohlenhof* has become the Austrians' show place and shop window for Haflinger breeding and training activities.

The International Haflinger Show is also held every five years at the *Fohlenhof*. Competitors travel from many countries in the world, including as far away as Australia, to take part in this prestigious event. A highlight of the show is the appearance of different family groups from the main stallion lines. They are exhibited as a group headed by a stallion with both male and female progeny shown in generation order. Some groups are extremely large and when one realises that some mares have had as many as fifteen foals apiece and these foals also have progeny, this is not so surprising.

In addition to the more usual competitions, for a brief period during the 1940s a system of achievement tests for Haflingers was also devised. They were introduced after the war by the Federation of Austrian Haflinger Breeders. The tests comprised a pulling test where a load of 2000 kg was pulled over a distance of 1000 m, and a stride and trotting test, each of which were run over a 1000 m course. However, these tests were found to be unnecessarily exhausting (although the Haflingers did stand up well to them) and they were not considered to be of any use in determining selection criteria for breeding purposes as had been initially proposed, so by the 1950s they had been discontinued.

Besides performing successfully in the competitive arena, the Haflinger also takes part in many other equestrian activities. Its temperament makes it an ideal vaulting horse for children, especially in Europe where this sport is well established. In this

The Silvretta Haflinger display team includes vaulting in its programme.

country Haflingers are well suited for use in Riding for the Disabled, where again temperament is of great importance. Their strength and stamina also makes them very suitable as trekking ponies and for endurance riding. They take kindly to Western style riding and to side saddle, and have been trained for tandem riding where the rider of one horse drives another one in front. In fact a Haflinger can be trained to take part successfully in just about any equestrian activity, such is its versatility and desire to please. Basically, Haflingers love people and adapt readily to whatever activities their owners require of them.

In Britain today, Haflingers take part in almost every area of equestrian activity. They can measure up to the requirements of any owner, whether for hacking, driving, competition or farm work.

Haflingers are strong in harness; because of their conformation they are able to throw their weight into the collar and provide maximum pulling power in relation to their size, so it is only natural that driving has always been popular with Haflinger owners. In the 1970s and early 1980s when Haflingers were still becoming established in Britain, Mrs Susan Brittain made a considerable contribution in promoting

The mare Heidrun, driven by Mrs Susan Brittain.

Bernhard, driven by Gillian Walker, receives his award from Her Grace the Duchess of Devonshire at the 1988 British Breed Show.

Haflingers for driving, with her two excellent mares Foich Linnhe and Heidrun. They distinguished themselves on many occasions in both British Driving Society (BDS) affiliated classes and at the Haflinger Society of Great Britain Breed Show. A worthy successor to Mrs Brittain's mares appeared in the form of the stallion Bernhard. He was acquired by Judy Vigors in 1987 at the age of six years. Until that time he had been used only as a riding pony and he displayed a low head carriage and heaviness on the forehand, faults which do tend to be exhibited by Haflingers due to their somewhat stocky build. However, with careful and correct schooling, these faults can be eliminated and Bernhard in due course became supple and agile. He began competing in affiliated Private Driving classes against good quality competition and was consistently placed. Following these successes he went on to compete in Driving Trials where he also managed to get in the ribbons.

Tom Crane, the British society's Chairman since 1986, is also a driving enthusiast. His pair of Haflingers impressed everyone with the manner in which they led the Haflinger contingent through busy London streets without turning a hair during the Rotten Row Tercentenary Parade in Hyde Park in 1990. Tom also appears in the driving classes at the Breed Show as well as being one of the major British breeders; he runs the Oxnead Stud in Norfolk with his wife Susan. Although Tom is primarily a farmer he and Susan regularly breed quality youngstock including a number of colts who have subsequently passed inspection as stallions.

Another Haflinger who has made his mark in driving events is Cherry Chidwick's Harry. For a number of years, although Harry was competing in BDS Private Driving classes with considerable success both for Cherry and for her son Edward in Junior Whip classes, his breeding and registration could not be confirmed as he had become separated from his papers at an early age. Happily for Cherry and her family, sufficient evidence at last came to light to prove that Harry was actually Abergele St Patrick, and therefore a genuine purebred Haflinger. In 1990, driving Harry, Edward won a Junior Whip class which led to his being awarded the Stella Hancock Memorial Scholarship; and in 1993 with Cherry driving, Harry qualified for the Thimbleby and Shorland National Driving Championships, where he acquitted himself very well.

Another person who has done much over the years to encourage British Haflingers in the field of driving is Major Tom Coombs, a well-known whip and judge of driving events. Major Coombs is now one of the Society's vice presidents in recognition of his support when the Haflinger was a newcomer to the British equestrian scene.

In Suffolk Brownbread Story, better known as Merlin, is a familiar sight driving round the local lanes. He was originally bought in 1980 by Colin and Elisabeth Brotherton for their twelve-year-old daughter Lisa. Sadly, a year later Lisa died but

Merlin sets off with Santa Claus.

by that time Merlin was part of the family and Colin and Elisabeth were determined to keep him. Although their knowledge of horses was limited, with help from friends they learned fast and kept him initially for riding. After a few years they decided to break him to harness and over a period of time attended a number of events and shows where he always acquitted himself well, including the prestigious British Driving Society Show in the World Breeds Class. Nowadays in the summer he transports happy couples from church to wedding reception and appears at various local events. In the winter he pulls Santa's Sledge to please local children. Merlin has also been placed in classes at the BDS annual show at Windsor.

The present policy of breeding taller Haflingers with a more sloping shoulder is leading to improved action. The old butcher's pony type of spanking trot is giving way to a freer and more fluid action. As a result, there are now several Haflingers

Oxnead Aristocrat working on his dressage with rider/trainer Ann Birch.

Nomad, ridden by Emma
Kennet, about to enter
the arena at the 1993 Stallion
Parade at Stoneleigh.

competing with excellent results in affiliated dressage classes. Lesley Brown's stallion Oxnead Aristocrat, ridden by Ann Birch, is at present the most successful and he qualified in 1993 for the Addington Manor Elementary Regional Championships. In 1994 he began working at Medium and Advanced Medium level. In 1995 he qualified for the Medium Regional Dressage Championships and has begun working at Advanced level. By June 1995 he had amassed 182 BHS points. Helen Blair's stallion Nomad also has BHS points and is competing successfully, along with his stable companion Solfried, who has also made his mark in endurance riding. These three Haflingers, although regarded with some scepticism in dressage circles to begin with, have proved that they are just as good as the more usual horses competing in this discipline. Indeed they are yet another example not only of the Haflinger's versatility, but also of the breed's ability to achieve success in whatever they do. There are also other Haflinger owners who compete successfully in dressage at local level.

Over the last twenty or so years, riding has become recognised as excellent therapy for disabled people, both children and adults. The ponies used for this activity have to be very carefully selected with regard to both temperament and the ability to carry a considerable amount of weight. The Haflinger scores highly on both counts. Additionally, it is a size which is easy to mount and it has a smooth comfortable action with an easy rhythm which is ideal for the handicapped. Its friendly nature makes it especially endearing to adults and children alike and its unflappability in almost any situation makes it reliable and trustworthy for such a responsible task.

There are a number of Haflingers in Britain today that work regularly with Riding for Disabled groups. In particular, several of Mrs Julia Proctor's Haflingers have supported the Goodwood branch near Chichester for a number of years where they enjoy enormous popularity with their riders. Haflingers are also used in Scotland at the Camphill Rudolf Steiner School near Aberdeen. This school is the centre of the Camphill Movement which was founded in 1940 to provide education, community homes and therapeutic training for children, young people and adults. Riding therapy at the school began in the mid 1970s with one New Forest pony who was later joined by an Arab cross Connemara. Since then the Centre has experimented with the use of various different breeds until the conclusion was reached that Haflingers came out top every time. The centre is now planning to breed its own Haflingers.

A rather different use of Haflingers is demonstrated by Helen Blair's Silvretta Haflinger Display Team. In 1980 Helen visited Austria and was most impressed with the display activities she saw Haflingers taking part in there. She returned to

Members of the Silvretta Display Team at the British Breed Show.

Haflingers are brave; jumping through fire holds no fear.

Britain determined to produce a display team of her own which would be just as good as the Austrians'. From a small beginning at the Haflinger Breed Show where just two Haflingers put on a display which featured vaulting and jumping through hoops of fire, a very professional team has been established. By 1988 the team consisted of twelve ponies and riders and the display includes a parade, vaulting, riding and jumping. The finale is a spectacular twelve-abreast gallop across the arena. The riders are all dressed in brown, red and white, while the Haflingers, of course, all match anyway and give a smart and uniform appearance. The Display Team performs regularly throughout the summer at a variety of shows and fetes, including the Breed Show. The team promotes the Haflinger's versatility and gives much enjoyment both to those participating and to their audience.

A sport for which the Haflinger has proved to be eminently suitable is endurance riding. It is only fairly recently that this equestrian discipline has gained popularity other than as an activity run by the Arab Horse Society. It is an excellent way to combine a new challenge with the improvement of one's horsemanship. An integral part of the competition is the welfare of the horses taking part and consequently there is qualified veterinary surveillance throughout. Haflingers have tremendous stamina and although they cannot always produce the speeds of some of the other breeds, they will keep going while others fall by the wayside. Haflingers compete regularly in rides from twenty-mile Pleasure Rides to some of the major events in the endurance riding calendar. Because of Solfried's early success in endurance events, constant pressure was put on the authorities by his owner Helen Blair, which actually resulted in the breakthrough which altered the rules to allow animals under 14.2 hh to compete in the 100-mile rides. Helen and Solfried have won gold at the prestigious Golden Horseshoe Ride on Exmoor and placed fourth in the Summer Solstice One Day Race Ride, also receiving the trophy for the first ever pony to finish this race and the much-coveted Best Condition award. In 1992 Pendavey Matra and Alex Nix, already runners up in the British Junior Championship, were selected to represent Great Britain at a race ride in Exloo, Holland. It is believed that this was the first Haflinger ever to represent Great Britain. In 1994 he again represented Great Britain as a member of the Junior team, competing this time in Switzerland. On this occasion he was ridden by Chris Pell. In 1995 the stallion Bernhard began competing in endurance riding and within only months had upgraded from a novice to Gold Standard.

On a more individual basis, Jane Dotchin from Hexham in Northumberland has devised her own style of long distance riding. For many years now the autumn has seen her setting out with her Haflinger Jester, loaded with saddlebags and dog Piglet, to undertake rides throughout the British Isles lasting many weeks and covering hundreds of miles. Their exploits demonstrate further what an equable and adaptable chap the Haflinger is. She published a book some years ago entitled *Journeys through England with a Pack Pony* about some of her experiences. An extract from an article about one of her more recent rides through the Highlands of Scotland follows:

Each autumn I seem to load up Jester, my Haflinger gelding, with an amazing amount of equipment for our yearly trip . . . Jester was brought up to take on the role of pack pony from his brother Sitka, who had been my companion for nearly 20 years. Catherine Hanbury still has their mother, now well into her thirties. Sitka was her first foal and Jester her last. Haflingers seem to have an amazing capacity for understanding and adapting to one's ways. I have kept them for 26 years now. There is just something about them that gives them that bit extra. On this sort of trip they become a devoted companion and more like a friend as well as a willing servant . . . Jester and I usually cover about 30 miles a day at the beginning of the trip but they get proportionately less as the days get shorter . . .

One cold draughty night I gratefully accepted the shelter of a small caravan in the corner of a windswept field just South of Cumbernauld. Jester was tethered to the caravan hitch, but didn't settle. He missed the tent which he accepts as home – where I am. He knows if I leave it I always come back. Even loose in a large field he will never stray far from the tent and always lies down as near to it as possible. I have been woken up many times in the night by neighing and nickering from a dreaming pony! My sleep in the caravan that night was abruptly broken by a sudden thud and the whole caravan shuddering. I leapt up, grabbed a torch and peered through the door. No Jester – where was he? Only the end of a snapped rope remained attached to the caravan. A blast of cold air

Jester, loaded and ready to go, with Piglet the dog in the saddlebag.

Jane Dotchin and Jester enter Inverness.

hit me as I stepped out and shone the torch around. The reflection of two eyes met me in the beam of light. He wasn't far away but something had frightened him and he was most unwilling to come back to the caravan . . .

[Later on we took] a right of way through the Grampian Mountains [which] . . . winds through the hills for 27 miles. Most of it is Land Rover type of track but one part in the middle most definitely is not. On an earlier trip when I used it, it had been so boggy that Jester had sunk right down to his belly . . . Jester remembered when we reached the expanse of soft peat and he put his brakes on very firmly. I dismounted and he reluctantly followed behind as I carefully picked a way trying to find firm ground . . . There were some hair raising moments when what had seemed like firm ground suddenly gave way under Jester's weight but each time he managed to regain his footing and we made it safely round the boggy area back onto the track . . .

[On the return journey] the weather suddenly changed to winter and we camped on snow at Tomintoul. There was a couple of feet of snow over the Lecht and all the ski lifts were operating, much to Jester's amazement. His eyes popped out on stalks at the sight of them whizzing down the snowy slopes and then being towed back up again.

Once away from the Cairngorms the snow receded but we had severe frosts at night all the way home. Jester thrived on carrots, oatmeal and whatever grass he could scavenge and judging by his stomach, looked as though he never lost much weight! He also had a waterproof cover to wear at night. The last hundred miles or so were a battle against gales, rain, sleet and snow, but we seemed to thrive and it hasn't dampened our spirits. Hopefully we are off to Ireland next autumn – it can really rain there, but at least it is warmer rain than in Scotland!

On a working level Haflingers also make their contribution. In Sussex, Langford Strida earns his keep by harrowing the pony paddocks on the farm where he lives. This keeps him in trim for his annual visit to the Agricultural Activity Weekend at the Weald and Downland Open Air Museum at Singleton. He was first invited there some years ago to demonstrate that in medieval times, before the more modern heavy horses were bred, it was ponies who carried out much of the farm work. Now, Strida holds his own alongside the Big Boys!

In Derbyshire, a Haflinger mare and a New Forest gelding are used on an eighteen-acre smallholding for all the work which would normally be done by a tractor. They plough, roll, harrow, cart muck, pull logs and do any other jobs which need carrying out. They even won the cup at a nearby ploughing match for the Best Locals. Not bad for a 13.2 hh pair!

As well as being prominent among British breeders, Helen Blair and Zena Fielding both use Haflingers in their thriving riding and driving centres. The Haflinger's quiet temperament is ideal for beginners in both disciplines, while his desire to belong endears him to younger riders who love to participate in such activities as 'Own a Pony' day in their school holidays.

Haflingers make ideal trekking ponies too. In Scotland a local trekking centre has used nothing but Haflingers for the last fifteen years. Ponies are considered the best type of all-round animal for use with both adults and children. The problem is that when some riders weigh as much as eighteen stone, a very strong pony is needed, yet as children are also among the clients, that strength must be tempered with docility, and here the Haflinger temperament comes into its own. They willingly carry any sort of rider, old, young, large or small and are ideally suited to both novice and more experienced riders. Even disabled riders have been able to join some of the treks.

In short, given the appropriate training and care, a Haflinger is capable of holding its own in whatever equestrian sphere one might wish to participate in.

Haflingers in Britain

There are approximately 500 living Haflingers in Great Britain in the mid 1990s, although about 1000 have actually been registered in the thirty or so years since they first made their appearance here. The first Haflinger did not arrive in the country until 1962, and it was the latter part of that decade before they began to appear in any significant numbers.

The first group of Haflingers was imported into Britain by the Roberts family in 1962, and comprised a stallion, Adler II, and several mares to form a small stud. Phyllis Roberts subsequently wrote an enthusiastic piece on the Haflinger, which appeared in the 1963 Pony Club Book. The mares did produce a number of foals but unfortunately the original buyers dispersed this stud quite early on, so that it did not really make the firm start to the establishment of the breed here which Mrs Roberts had clearly hoped to do when she wrote her article. The stallion was sold on the Welsh markets and vanished completely, although a trophy was later presented to the Breed Show for the stallion breed class in his memory. The mares were sold separately, the two most notable of which being Borga and Udina. Some stock from these two mares has continued into the present bloodlines. Udina, who was imported in foal to the Austrian stallion Notker, produced the stallion Notangus, while Borga has an ongoing mare line. Udina, Notangus and the four-year-old Borga were purchased in 1963 by Catherine Hanbury. Borga was still alive in 1995 and believed to be the oldest Haflinger in the country. However, Notangus was assessed as a stallion before the criteria for the British stud book and inspection system had been laid down; in 1971 when Herr Schweisgut visited his owner's stud to inspect some mares he also looked at Notangus and downgraded him to Section B because he disapproved of the white markings on the stallion's legs. In the meantime the British stud book had been set up and Section B stallions were not acceptable for registration. In fact Section B blood, even in the dam, is unacceptable anywhere in a stallion's ancestry. Notangus' line therefore could not continue in the main stud book. He was mostly used on a Norwegian Fjord mare, the only two pure Haflinger mares he covered being Borga and her first daughter Berry.

There was another importation in the mid 1960s which consisted of a group of animals from an Austrian trekking centre which had closed down. Three of these mares, Sissi, Tilly and Heidi I produced foals, although their lines seem to have disappeared now.

In 1967 Anne Rolinson (née Hammond) became interested in the breed. She has given the following account of her introduction to Haflingers:

In January 1967 I was approached by Herr Schweisgut who was contemplating purchasing an Arab stallion to re-introduce Arabian blood into the Haflinger Stud Book. He specified the necessity for a chestnut horse with a blaze but no white markings on the legs, and a pure flaxen mane and tail. After research and many enquiries I located three possible stallions which Otto Schweisgut came to see in the spring, although later he decided against the project.

As a direct result of my involvement, Herr Schweisgut invited me to Austria that summer to be shown the Haflinger horses in their native country based at Innsbruck. This involved not only a visit to the *Fohlenhof* at Ebbs, but also the unique opportunity to accompany Herr Schweisgut on the Inspections, often to remote villages and farms in the Tyrol, meeting the breeders and seeing the Haflinger stallions owned by the Society but allocated to stand with stud owners or farmers in different regions of the Tyrol. I was very impressed to see how quiet and well mannered most of the horses were at these 'Stallion Stations'. At this time Haflinger mares could be seen working between shafts, some even having their foals beside them while hauling large loads of hay.

The uniformity of type and consistent attractive chestnut colouring of the breed together with their strength and soundness plus the generally calm sensible temperament made a lasting impression on me. I returned home with many happy memories of the kindness and hospitality shown me by Haflinger owners and breeders in the Tyrol and a treasured signed copy of Herr Schweisgut's book of the Haflinger horse, with an inscription in German which when translated 'wished that I might return soon to buy my first Haflinger horses'. Within a few months several friends had become interested and enthusiastically supported my idea of importing a small number of Haflinger mares for the benefit of Riding for the Disabled groups and potential breeders. As a direct result of that I was able to return to Austria and select the initial group of Haflinger mares.

In May 1968 Anne organised a major importation of five mares and two two-year-old fillies. Although some of these lines have now died out, two of the mares established good lines to follow them. Hermi, who went to Scotland, bred a number of foals including two good daughters. The first of these daughters, Heidi II, has in her turn bred more good quality animals. The other mare, Marika, also established a strong female line through her daughter Edial Mercedes.

One of the two-year-old fillies, Lispa, was purchased by Her Grace the Duchess of Devonshire, who became very interested in Haflingers from the early days and established a Haflinger Stud at Chatsworth. This mare bred some excellent quality stock for the Duchess. Her Grace had seen and been impressed by Haflingers in the popular Group Costume Class at the Ponies of Britain Show at Peterborough in 1968 or 1969, when Anne Rolinson's (then Anne Hammond) Millfields Riding Establishment entry had an Austrian theme. This included Marika driven to a Pickering Float, and Ridi and Carola (two of the 1968 imported mares) with their foals, surrounded by a group of children dressed in Tyrolean costumes and accompanied by Edda Binder from Innsbruck (the enthusiastic secretary and interpreter to Herr Schweisgut), who was on holiday in England and had brought the colourful costumes with her and had also provided authentic background music with her Austrian tapes. The Duchess of Devonshire's reason for importing Haflingers was the necessity for a small work horse with good strength and the right temperament to use for hauling timber on the steep slopes of the estate at Chatsworth. The Duchess had previously run a highly successful Shetland pony stud and together with Mr Jones, her experienced stud groom, was very enthusiastic about the new project, and the Haflinger Stud at Chatsworth was soon established. It was an ideal background to see not only the mares and foals, but also the Haflinger in harness, working in the woods on the Chatsworth estate.

The other two year old imported in 1968, Schatzel, was chosen for Jane Evers-Swindell (who became the British Chief Inspector in 1986) and has two strong mare lines flourishing through her daughters Evers Schön and Evers Schwan. Schön was purchased by Margaret Leach and became famous as the dam of four stallions – Coombe Wood Stolz, Stumper, Strahl and Niko. She also has a very strong ongoing mare line through her daughters Coombe Wood Schona and Schayla. Schona's two daughters were both exported and one, Scharma, has already produced two champion fillies in France.

Also in 1968, Margaret Davenport imported two mares, Lola and Sisia, and a W-line stallion, Waldo, from Holland. Both the mares bred some good stock and Sisia's line should be continued by her daughter Oxnead Signoretta, who has a strong line continuing through her daughter Oxnead Sapphire. Sapphire's promising daughter Oxnead Sadie was exported to the USA in 1993.

The year 1969 contained important milestones for Haflingers in Britain. First of all the Austrian government presented two mares, Franzi and Trista, to Her Majesty the Queen when she was on a state visit to Austria. Although Trista has no descendants to continue her line, she did breed a gelding. Franzi bred a daughter Balmoral Freya,

Presentation of Franzi and Trista to Her Majesty the Queen in Vienna, 1969.

who it was hoped might also be bred from; however, although she is still living, she is perhaps too old now to have a first foal. Freya has been stabled at the Silvretta Stud since 1993 and in 1994 she celebrated her twenty-first birthday. She has taken part in some long distance rides and Her Majesty continues to take an interest in her progress and well-being. In the 1970s HRH Prince Philip drove a team of four Haflingers competitively and Haflingers were also used on the estate at Balmoral for trekking and timber hauling.

The other events of significance in 1969 were two large importations of stock, including the first two stallions to be registered in the British stud book. The three-year-old stallion Stormer went to Ernie Holmes' Wrekin Stud together with a number of mares, in May. In December Anne Rolinson returned to Austria at the behest of the Duchess of Devonshire and imported the stallion Maximilian along with several mares, including Verena and Texas who both have continuing lines, on behalf of the Duchess. At the same time Anne also brought in other mares who went to Margaret Davenport's Sandy Stud in Bedfordshire and to the Evers Stud in North Wales. Putz, imported in foal to Westwind, produced the stallion Evers Waldchen.

Stormer, shown by Ernie Holmes, at the Royal Show, 1978.

Maximilian at the first Breed Show, held at Chatsworth in 1971.

By the 1970s, interest in the Haflingers in Britain was increasing steadily and although quite a large number of British foals were now being bred, there were still nowhere near enough animals to meet the demand. The 1970s proved to be a peak time for importing stock from Austria. The Countess of Chichester became interested in the breed and imported the stallion Strudl, by Steinadler, together with a mare. Andre Matysiak imported the stallion Anderson as a foal along with some half a dozen mares. Angela Dewhurst returned from the Tyrol with the stallion Monar and four mares, while the Duchess of Devonshire also imported further mares, including Eger-Elsa, for her stud at Chatsworth. Ernie Holmes of the Wrekin stud imported additional mares, and other enthusiasts attended several of the *Fohlenhof* sales and came back with a selection of youngstock. Andre Matysiak imported more fillies, including Kandida who, as well as having a very strong ongoing mare line, was also the dam of two stallions, Devon Novara and Devon Adler. Mrs Eleanor Kerr imported the mare Olfa in 1972 and the following year Mrs Hutley purchased Jeramie, full sister to the important Austrian stallion liz. Afghan, and the top priced filly at the Ebbs Foal Sale that year. Unfortunately Jeramie disappeared for a long time and was eventually found in the late 1980s in a run-down riding school in Wiltshire. She was purchased in poor condition for a fraction of the sum which she had originally fetched and her purchaser at that stage had no idea how important she had been. It

Anderson was not broken to harness until he was eighteen years of age. Seen here driven at the 1993 Stallion Parade.

was realised that she had previously foaled and when a decision was made to put her in foal once more in 1993, she was taken to the stallion Coombe Wood Stolz with the result that Jeramie was recognised as one of the 'lost' Haflingers. She produced a colt foal in 1994 but sadly died when the foal was just a couple of months old. The owners hand-reared the foal and there are hopes that it may reach the required standard for a stallion, as the mare's bloodlines were impeccable.

By the 1980s the great flood of imports had slowed down as more Haflingers were now being bred in Britain. There were representatives of all the stallion lines with the exception of the B-line and N-line by the end of the 1970s – even the rare S-line was represented at that time by Foich Schiechallion, bred from an in-foal mare imported by Angela Dewhurst and later sold to Margaret Davenport. During the 1980s stallions from the two lines not previously represented were brought into the country. The B-line stallion Bernhard was imported by Norman Davidson and later acquired

Bernhard, sired by the Austrian stallion Brutus who was sold to Germany.

by Judy Vigors. In 1986 Judy imported two N-line colts from France. One, Nomad, is now registered as a stallion. Bernhard was sold to Northern Ireland in 1992 as stud stallion for a Mr Taylor. However, in the summer of 1994 Judy Vigors happened to be visiting Northern Ireland and found Mr Taylor had died and no one seemed to know what to do with the Haflingers. Judy immediately arranged for them to be shipped back to England where they have since been sold on to several different breeders, Bernhard being purchased by Helen Blair. The last of the imports of this decade was made in 1989 by Tom and Susan Crane, who brought in another A-line stallion, Alpine, to inject some fresh blood into their Oxnead Stud.

In the summer of 1990, June Gillis and her family returned to England from Germany where they had lived for some years, bringing with them three mares and

Alpine, shown by Emily Dewing at the Breed Show, 1994.

Nelson is one of the younger British stallions. His first crop of foals will be due for inspection in 1997.

some quality youngstock. Although these animals were technically German bred, they are actually from good Austrian lines which had been imported by the Germans. One of these, the colt Nelson, has now been registered as a British stallion. In September 1990 several people attended the autumn sale at the *Fohlenhof* and another half a dozen fillies were purchased.

Today, Haflinger breeding is flourishing in Great Britain. At the 1993 youngstock inspections two stallions and ten mares were accepted for registration in the stud book. In 1994, three stallions were passed, all sired by Alpine, and a number of mares were also registered. Sadly, however, only four stallion lines are represented in Britain at the time of writing – the A-line, the B-line (with Bernhard's return), the N-line and the ST-line. Nevertheless, thirteen stallions were available at stud in 1994:

Alpine, Oxnead Adam, Oxnead Alpha, Garway Aladdin, Anderson, Oxnead Aristocrat, Nelson, Coombe Wood Niko, Nomad, Chevin Stollen, Coombe Wood Stolz, Coombe Wood Strahl and Strudl. Stormer, who at the age of twenty-seven was the oldest stallion in Britain and was still serving his mares at the Wrekin Stud in 1993, died in 1994.

The remaining stallions are producing good stock and it is hoped that Nelson and Niko, the two stallions registered in 1993, together with Adam, Alpha and Aladdin

Coombe Wood Niko.

who passed inspection in 1994, will all prove to be first-class sires. Nelson covered selected mares in 1993, and his first foals appeared in 1994. Niko did not cover any mares until 1994 so his first progeny were only seen in 1995.

The original stallions brought into this country from Austria all had excellent pedigrees but unfortunately not all these lines seem likely to continue. Maximilian, whose line traces back to Nilo through Marius and liz. Stürmer, sired five more stallions, but despite this apparent proliferation his line now appears to have died out. Stormer belonged to the Stromer branch of the ST-line through his grandsire, Strom. He sired three stallions and his line may yet continue through his son Coombe Wood Stolz and his grandson Chevin Stollen who is now standing in Scotland. Monar, whose line can be traced back to Nilo through Mordskerl, produced one stallion, Oxnead Majesty, who was exported to Canada as a youngster. His line may continue through his son Malachi, now standing in the USA. Anderson has an impeccable pedigree, being the son of Artist and half brother to liz. Afghan. He has sired two stallions to date, both of which were later gelded, although not before Oxnead Ambassador had sired Oxnead Aristocrat who may yet keep the line going. Anderson of course is still at stud himself. Strudl, the other ST-line stallion imported in the early 1970s, belongs to the Steinadler branch. He has sired two stallions and his line will hopefully continue in this country through Coombe Wood Strahl, who at seven years old would seem to have a promising future. His first son, Coombe Wood Stumper, was sold to France where he later became European Champion. Unfortunately, Evers Waldchen, out of the mare Putz who was imported in foal to Westwind, was later gelded when he failed to live up to his earlier promise and has no line to follow him. Nomad, a later import from France, has already sired Coombe Wood Niko who is now registered as a stallion, so his line could be set to continue. Bernhard, a son of Brutus imported from Germany, sired the stallion Clifton Brunel (exported to the USA) before he himself went to Ireland. His line, too, could continue. Alpine's first crop of foals were presented for inspection as three-year-olds in 1994 and the indications are that to date he is throwing excellent quality stock, as three of his offspring were accepted into the stud book as stallions that year. Nelson's first foals arrived in 1994 and Coombe Wood Niko had his first season at stud in 1994.

Attempts are being made to reintroduce some of the missing stallion lines, although the Austrians are naturally reluctant to sell their best stock outside Austria. One British breeder took mares to Ebbs in 1993 to be covered by top Austrian stallions, which resulted in a W-line colt by Winterstein being born in 1994; the breeder hopes it will make the grade as a stallion when it comes up for inspection in 1997. Fillies are still being imported, although the cost of bringing new lines into the country is becoming higher and higher, so it is important that British-bred stock continues to be of excellent quality and that the good mare lines are preserved.

Unfortunately a number of good mare lines which were included in those early imports have been lost. There are various reasons for this. In some cases mares have been sold on to people who were not interested in breeding; others were sold on without their papers being transferred and after changing hands several times they can no longer be identified; yet others proved to be barren or tragically died before producing a filly foal. However, there still remain some mares from those who were among the good quality early imports which do have strong ongoing female lines.

Verena, who belonged to the Duchess of Devonshire, was the first mare to be registered in the British stud book. Her line is continuing at present through her first daughter Chatsworth Veronica, but if her great granddaughter Clifton Victoria fails to produce daughters, this line will die out. Hety, imported by Ernie Holmes, produced seven daughters and her line is flourishing through Wrekin Helga and Helga's daughters. Hermi I has a strong line continuing through her daughter Heidi, who produced two stallions and several daughters. These daughters have in turn produced further daughters to continue the line.

Schatzel has already been mentioned as an important foundation mare. Her sire, Stüber, was the foundation stallion of the modern ST-line in the Tyrol. Her daughters Schwan and Schon have bred a number of daughters and their stock can be found in the USA, France and Northern Ireland as well as in Britain. Putz has an ongoing line through her daughter Evers Patience, who has three daughters and one granddaughter.

Eger-Elsa, another of the Duchess of Devonshire's early imports, was a Stüber granddaughter from the excellent Austrian Albina-Lucy mare strain. She produced six daughters and her line is flourishing through her first daughter Chatsworth Eliza, who produced the stallion Chevin Stollen and two daughters, one of whom has already bred a champion daughter who will in due course also be used for breeding.

Olfa was imported by the Kerrs in foal to Iiz. Afghan and produced a filly, Silverton Oriana, who in turn produced the stallion Silverton Noury and four filly foals. One of the latter, Silverton Ottilia, has a ongoing line – her first daughter Garway Orchid produced a colt foal, New Yorker, in 1994 and a filly, Olwyn, in 1995. Silverton Ottilia is also the dam of Garway Aladdin.

Nina, based at Oxnead, bred the former stallion Oxnead Ambassador who was the sire of the stallion Oxnead Aristocrat. Nina's line is continuing strongly through her daughters Oxnead Nobell, Nania and Natalie.

Finally, of those early imports, Kandida's line is part of one of the most important

Austrian mare strains. She is a great great granddaughter of Kalterer-Moid, the famous liz. Stürmer daughter. Besides being the dam of two stallions, Kandida has bred several daughters to continue her own line, which is considered valuable and should be preserved if possible.

There are thus still many quality animals in the country and, with an upsurge in both breeding and demand, the Haflinger population of Britain looks set to increase during the 1990s. Several of the breeders believe in the Austrian principles of careful line breeding and the Haflinger Society of Great Britain has based its policy and standards on that of the World Haflinger Federation, whose rules follow those set by the Austrians. The Society encourages the British breeders to follow these principles.

In 1970, following the two large consignments of Haflingers which had been imported in 1969, the Duchess of Devonshire and Anne Rolinson realised that if proper records were not quickly put together and kept up to date, a great deal of important information would be permanently lost. In July 1970 the Duchess therefore invited Otto Schweisgut and his son to come to England and speak to a small gathering of people who had shown interest in Haflingers. This led to the inaugural meeting of the Haflinger Society of Great Britain which was held at Chatsworth on 17 November 1970. Otto Schweisgut also attended this meeting together with the secretary of the *Haflinger Zuchtverband Tirol*, Fraulein Edda Binder. Besides the Duchess of Devonshire and Anne Rolinson, proprietor of a registered riding establishment and Connemara stud, a number of people already prominent in the pony world also supported the Haflinger – most notably Mrs Yeomans, Mrs Bromiley and Mrs Tollitt, who were all respected judges in the pony world.

At that first meeting a committee was elected, comprising the Duchess of Devonshire as Chairman, Anne Rolinson as Vice Chairman and Jane Evers-Swindell as Secretary/Treasurer. Elected committee members were Miss C. Hanbury, who ran a Northumberland riding centre and was already a Haflinger breeder, Mr E. Holmes of the Wrekin stud, Mrs M. Bromiley, and Mrs I. Yeomans. At the meeting the rules and objectives were set for the Society, which were 'To promote and extend the breeding of Haflingers in Great Britain; and to advise and assist persons and authorities interested in breeding and exhibiting Haflingers.' The Society also proposed to keep proper records and adopt the strict Austrian policy of inspecting all stock and rejecting for registration that which did not meet the required standards. The Austrians agreed to help with the recording until the British animals numbered 500. Margaret Davenport remembers the Society's first annual subscription being set at just seven shillings and sixpence!

In July 1971 the first Breed Show was held at Chatsworth. More than thirty animals

The first British Haflinger Breed Show was held at Chatsworth in 1971.

were exhibited and there was considerable interest from the public. One of the ponies which attended was Jane Dotchin's original long distance pony, Sitka. Herr Schweisgut gave the Society great encouragement by attending the show and he also inspected and branded some Haflingers. The ponies were then tied up in specially erected stalls so that the public could walk round and see them properly. The first Annual General Meeting of the Society was held in November 1971, by which time fifty-five Haflingers had been accepted for registration in the British stud book. In that year sixteen foals had been born.

Also during the early 1970s the Society took display stands for several years at the Royal Show, following which the show included classes for Haflingers. Usually a stallion, a mare and foal and a barren mare were put on display and this form of advertising proved to be a very successful way of introducing the Haflinger to the British public and of promoting the breed in its early days here. A number of people became Haflinger owners as a result of first seeing the breed at the Royal Show. More recently the Society has taken a stand at the British Equine Event held at Stoneleigh in November and considerable interest has been shown in the breed on these occasions. The Society returned to the Royal Show with a stand in 1994 and 1995.

In 1982 Britain acted as host for the World Haflinger Federation Meeting, which was held in conjunction with the Annual Breed Show at Chatsworth. It brought delegates from all over the world, many of whom also attended the Breed Show. Herr Schweisgut again judged some of the classes.

The Tercentenary of Rotten Row in Hyde Park was celebrated in 1990. One of the events organised for this occasion was a parade of horses and ponies; any clubs, groups or individuals were invited to take part. It was an event at which the Society felt the Haflinger should be represented. Accordingly a pair of mares, driven by Tom Crane, the Society's chairman, and eight ridden ponies travelled to London to take part in the parade. The Haflingers, with their uniform and striking appearance,

Tom Crane, driving the mares which led the Haflinger contingent at the Tercentenary of Rotten Row.

attracted considerable attention and were quickly christened the 'Haflinger Cavalry' by one of the stewards! All of them behaved impeccably despite the many strange sights and sounds, including the London buses.

During the late 1970s and early 1980s, Sir Eric Pountain as chairman did a great deal to put the Society on a sound footing. His former company, Tarmac, have provided generous sponsorship for a number of years. Sir Eric also bred some good stock at his Edial stud and ensured the Society continued in the spirit in which it had been started. Since 1986 the chairman has been Tom Crane and he works very hard to guide the Society in the 1990s to ensure that standards are kept in line with those set by the Austrians and the World Haflinger Federation. It is very encouraging to note that a number of the founder members still play an active part in the Society, with the Duchess of Devonshire retaining an interest as Patron and Sir Eric Pountain retaining his connection as President.

Inspection of the British Haflinger is carried out in accordance with very similar standards to those laid down by the Austrians. The pony is first measured for height and bone, and then a drawing is made of markings and whorls and a written description given of colour of the body, mane and tail. The inspector will then assess the pony on a scale of 1 to 10 for the various parts of the body. The following is a rough guide as to how the points are allocated in each section:

> 10   Never given
> 9   Excellent (*all* 9s are never given)
> 8   Good quality
> 7   Normal/Average
> 6   Bad/Poor
> 5   Fail (2 sections marked at 5 = Fail)
> 1 – 4   Fail

The guide for overall type is:

> 10   Never given
> 9   Elegant lightly built riding type with good movement and withers
> 8   Lighter type with some quality
> 7   Medium/heavy type
> 6   Very heavy type

The final points are given for the overall quality of the animal, which includes consideration of colour (white markings, other than a star or blaze, are frowned upon and, while not a point in themselves for failure, can influence the overall quality mark) and movement. At this point the temperament is also taken into account, which for the Haflinger must be excellent as it is an important aspect of the breed. The points are totalled and, together with the height of the pony, determine which section of the stud book the animal is entered in.

A panel of two or three inspectors, headed by Jane Evers-Swindell, carries out the inspections which as far as possible take place at the Stallion Parade in March each year. Inspectors need to have considerable general knowledge of horses and judging

Jane Evers-Swindell takes a break from inspecting.

73

plus particular knowledge of the Haflinger. Before an inspector is fully recognised, he or she must undergo several years' training alongside the experienced inspectors. The Society also has a panel of trained Haflinger judges.

The table shows points and classifications together with the Austrian equivalents. Section B is the lowest category recognised for entry in the British stud book. In Austria Class III, the equivalent of Section B, is not acceptable for registration.

Stallions, in addition to meeting all the above requirements, must be a minimum height of 13.3 hh (140 cm) on inspection at three years old and are expected to grow at least a further 1.5 inches (4 cm). Bone measurement must be at least 7.25 inches (18.4 cm). Stallions will not even be considered for inspection unless their dam is at least 13.1¹/₄ (135 cm). No Section B blood is acceptable anywhere in its parentage. Since 1993 all stallions also have had to be blood typed before they can be fully registered and permitted to stand at stud.

Stallions, and mares which pass inspection, are then branded on the left flank with the Eidelweiss brand, which is the same as that used in Austria.

In Britain, colts which are not eligible for consideration as stallions, or which fail inspection as a stallion, must be gelded and will then be entered in the gelding register. A gelding does not have to be inspected for entry to the gelding register. If the owner/breeder considers a colt will not meet the standards required for a stallion, it may be gelded and entered in the gelding register at any age. Geldings are not branded other than as foals when they should be marked on their left shoulder with the shoulder brand, which is the letter 'H' surmounted by the initials 'GB'. All foals should receive this brand which identifies them as British Haflingers. They are also issued with a continuous stud book number at this stage, which should later be changed either to their registered mare or stallion number or their gelding stud book number, as appropriate.

As in Austria, male offspring are always named with the first letter of their sire's name and female offspring are named with that of their dam. All animals are given stud book numbers, even the geldings, but these are not always used, as in Austria, as part of the animal's identification except in the stud book. For general identification purposes the breeder's prefix is normally included as part of the name, so even where ponies bear the same name, the breeder's prefix will distinguish one from another.

Inspections in Britain are carried out by a dedicated team of inspectors led by Jane Evers-Swindell. The main inspections are now carried out in March at the Stallion Parade, but the inspectors can also visit individual studs if required. Jane has been involved with the Haflinger Society in Britain since the very beginning and was the

	British Class	Austrian Class	Points	Height
Section A	1	Ib+	85 and more	13.3+/140cm
	1	Ib	83 - 84	13.3+/140cm
	1	Ib-	81 - 82	13.3+/140cm
	2	IIa+	79 - 80	13.2-/138cm
	2	IIa	77 - 78	13.2-/138cm
	2	IIa-	75 - 76	13.2-/138cm
	3	IIb+	73 - 74	13.1¼/135cm
	3	IIb	71 - 72	13.1¼/135cm
	3	IIb-	66 - 70	13.1¼/135cm
	4	III	60 - 65	13.1¼/135cm
Section B	5	—	50 or more	—
	6	—	20 or more	—

Classification table of grades given at inspection.

Society's first Secretary/Treasurer. She and her family became involved with Haflingers after seeing a travel programme on Austria in 1968 which featured some pretty ponies with flaxen manes and tails quietly grazing in the background. The family wrote to Herr Otto Schweisgut to enquire about obtaining some of these ponies and were put in touch with Anne Rolinson who had already purchased some. Jane has been a judge and inspector for many years, and since 1986, Chief Inspector. She has spent a great deal of time in Austria studying the Haflinger and the Austrian methods and standards of inspection and has been invited to judge in Austria, which is the highest accolade the Austrians can award to a foreigner. Jane also rides, and competes with her Haflingers at the Breed Show and other shows during the season. She has taken part in just about every equine discipline possible from jumping to gymkhanas, and dressage to hunter trials with successes in all activities. Throughout the Haflinger world Jane is held in great respect.

Right from the very early days there have been several extremely enthusiastic Haflinger breeders in Britain, but despite this there has always been difficulty in producing enough animals to meet the demand. There always seems to be a shortage of mature, schooled ponies available for riding and driving. The Haflinger, once seen, appears to gain instant popularity. As has already been mentioned, the Duchess of Devonshire was one of the earliest breeders and did a great deal in the 1970s to put the Haflinger on the map in Britain. Her stud at Chatsworth produced some very good stock, sired by her stallion Maximilian. Ernie Holmes was another of the early breeders and is still in business today at his Wrekin Stud in Shropshire. Jane Evers-Swindell breeds from time to time from her favourite mares in North Wales. Other breeders from those early days were Miss Catherine Hanbury, owner of Borga (who at thirty-four years is believed to be the oldest living Haflinger in Britain), Mr and Mrs Norman Davidson, Sir Eric Pountain, Lt Col. and Mrs Patrick Brittain, Mrs Angela Dewhurst, Mr Andre Matysiak, Mr Wilf Higgins, Mr and Mrs Clemerson, Mrs Eleanor Kerr and the Countess of Chichester. Margaret Davenport still keeps Haflingers and remains an active member of the Society.

The stallion owners are among the more prominent Haflinger breeders in Britain today and there are studs spread across a wide area of the country. Tom and Susan Crane (who in 1989 purchased the stallion Alpine, imported from Austria) breed from the Oxnead Stud in Norfolk. Lesley Brown, whose stallion Oxnead Aristocrat (bred by the Cranes) stands at her Stagsden Stud near Bedford, is breeding several foals each year. Christine Richmond's stallion Chevin Stollen stands at the Bekon Stud, which recently moved to Scotland. Helen Blair owns the stallions Nomad and Bernhard and runs the Silvretta Stud in the West Midlands. Margaret Leach owns Coombe Wood Stolz and breeds in Somerset. Her other stallion, Coombe Wood Strahl, was sold to Joanne Critchlow in 1994. In 1990, Zena Fielding purchased the stallion Anderson (who celebrated his twenty-first birthday in 1994) and has also recently bought Coombe Wood Niko, a three-year-old stallion registered in 1993, to join Anderson and continue breeding at her Trecarric Stud in Cornwall. Ann Coppock, who has owned the stallion Strudl (another 'oldie') for a number of years now, breeds in Hereford and Ernie Holmes continued breeding from Stormer until the stallion died in 1994. Helen Robbins' Garway Haflingers near Bristol is producing good quality stock, including the stallion Aladdin who was registered in 1994. Cynthia Shingleton still breeds a foal from each of her two mares every year at the Chevin Stud in Derbyshire. Mrs Procter's Langford Haflingers are also thriving in Sussex as are Kristin Evans' Whitbourne Haflingers in Worcester. Judy Vigors' Cranbourne Stud was effectively dispersed in 1992 with the sale of Bernhard and

Oxnead Aristocrat demonstrates the Haflinger's versatility. Here he is shown under side saddle.

most of the mares. However, breeding is still continuing there on a much smaller scale with the mares which were retained. Two new breeders are June and Richard Gillis whose interest in Haflingers began when they lived in Germany. They brought Nelson, the other three-year-old stallion accepted into the stud book in 1993, and a number of good quality mares with them when they settled in South Wales with their family in 1990 as mentioned earlier. Their business is currently expanding and they now run two stallions, since Oxnead Alpha, which they bought as a two year old, passed inspection in 1994. Bernard Ehlen, whose Camphill-Steiner school has already been discussed, uses Haflingers for riding therapy and has recently settled in Scotland with the intention of breeding Haflingers there for use in the school.

A Breed Show has been held annually since the very early days of the Society. The first shows were held at Chatsworth, but later the locations varied, rather depending on who had accepted the task of organising the show. By 1989 the Breed Show had grown so much in size and in the variety of classes offered that a permanent show sub-committee was formed to run it. Since then the show has been held at the Three Counties Showground at Malvern each July.

Brownbread Story driven in Austrian style at Malvern.

The author's Haflinger, Wrekin Storli; an example of the older, chunkier Haflinger.

Other major shows which hold classes for Haflingers are the Royal Windsor, the Three Counties, the Midlands In Hand, and the Royal Show. Haflingers have been accepted in the Native Performance Show since 1993. Haflingers also compete with success in a wide variety of classes at local shows around the country.

The Breed Show and the Annual General Meeting are the Society's two main events each year when members can get together, on one occasion with their Haflingers and on the other without, to compare notes. For the last few years the Breed Show, which has benefited by generous sponsorship from Tarmac, has stretched over two days, making it an enjoyable weekend both for those showing their Haflingers and for members simply wishing to spectate and meet up again with their friends. An international Haflinger judge is normally invited to judge the breed classes at the Breed Show in order to avoid any possible claims of partiality. In the breed classes the continental way of showing in hand has now been adopted. It is a

The continental system of showing uses a triangle.

CONTINENTAL SHOWING TRIANGLE

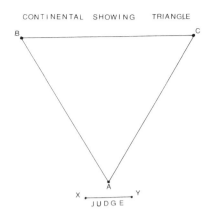

very good system since it gives the judge a better view of how an animal moves from all directions. The system is based on a triangle, marked only at the three corners, as in the diagram. The handler enters the ring and walks the pony from C to A towards the judge, halts and stands the animal up on the line X–Y, facing X, for initial assessment. The pony is then trotted away from A to B in order for the judge to watch the movement from behind. The pony stops at B, turns right and trots again to C while the judge assesses length of stride. It finally turns right again and trots back to A to the judge, to enable his movement to be assessed from the front.

The Annual General Meeting, which is held in October or November, is both a day for doing the Society's business and a social occasion. The business meeting takes place in the morning, followed by a lunch. In the afternoon general discussions and Brains Trusts have been held or videos shown.

Since 1989 the Society has held an annual Stallion Parade with youngstock inspections in March. While this is the main 'shop window' for the stallion owners, other members are encouraged to attend and it is an interesting and enjoyable day. This activity began in a small way at Helen Blair's yard, but by 1993 had outgrown those beginnings and moved on to the National Equestrian Centre at Stoneleigh, where it is hoped that it will continue with the same success with which it began.

From time to time regional groups have also been started up and various activities organised for members. One of the main problems with this type of Society is the fact that members often live so far apart from one another and the distances prevent frequent meetings. Unfortunately the success of these groups seems to fluctuate.

80

Currently the ones in the north of England and eastern England are thriving, while those in the south east and south west are not so active.

The policy of the Society will continue to be that of promoting the Haflinger as strongly and widely as possible and it is hoped that the breed will ultimately be given the same opportunities as, and chances to compete with, the British Mountain and Moorland breeds. At the present time there is some reluctance on the part of the National Pony Society, Ponies UK and breeders of British native ponies to accept breeds which are not native to this country, despite the fact that the Haflinger's ancestry as a mountain breed can be traced back for a number of centuries. Even though Haflinger breeding has been more scientifically controlled than some other native breeds over the last 120 or so years, there are very few truly wild native ponies anywhere today, and all the British Mountain and Moorland breeds are now bred for a large part on studs under man-made conditions. With the development of the European Union there surely has to be a place for all the native breeds of Europe to receive equal recognition throughout the continent.

The Society will also be making continued efforts to ensure that breeding standards are maintained and, if possible, improved, so that the quality of the ponies does not deteriorate. Recently there has been some controversy over the older working type of Haflinger as opposed to the modern type which is better developed for riding. Some people prefer the smaller more chunky animals which first came to Britain, and which were a legacy of the breeding carried out during the Second World War years, to the taller, finer quality animals that are being encouraged today. However, the demand is steadily increasing for riding ponies among adults as well as children, so provided the taller ponies do not lose bone and substance, the improved neck and shoulder will give them the greater length of stride more suitable for a riding horse. The British objectives remain in tune with those of the World Haflinger Federation, to breed a larger, better quality pony.

Having been in existence for over twenty years, the Haflinger Society of Great Britain is looking forward to celebrating its Silver Jubilee in 1996 and will then be hoping for another successful twenty-five years.

7 Haflingers worldwide

From its origins in the Tyrolean region of the Alps, the Haflinger breed has gradually been introduced to all five continents of the world. However, it is only since the 1950s that Haflingers have been found outside Europe. In fact, before the Second World War, the breed was only established in those countries with boundaries directly adjacent to the alpine region from whence it had originated.

Wherever in the world Haflingers have become established, it is interesting to note that they have quickly adapted to local climatic conditions and to whatever else was required of them by those who originally imported them. This adaptability must in some measure be attributed to their equable temperament and willing nature.

Europe

Italy

The South Tyrol in Italy was of course the original home of the Haflinger. Although it is the Austrians from the North Tyrol who have taken the lead in the development of the breed since the 1950s, the Italians too have made a not insignificant contribution. Unfortunately, however, before the 1970s the Italians had attempted to improve the breed more rapidly by carrying out a considerable amount of crossbreeding with Arabs and Thoroughbreds. As a result there are still a number of Haflingers in Italy which do not match up to the current standards of the World Haflinger Federation. Additionally, the Italian inspection standards do not yet fully conform to those followed by most other European countries, while their system of naming stallions by alpha characters representing a particular year rather than using the letter of the stallion line has also caused some confusion outside Italy. Nevertheless, breeding is flourishing in Italy today and currently there are some excellent quality Haflingers being bred.

Germany

Together with Italy and Austria, Germany was one of the earliest countries to see the potential of the Haflinger. Breeding became established in the 1930s when the

German Army was making considerable demands for the breed as a packhorse. After the end of the war when Germany was divided, Haflinger breeding developed in both East and West Germany, albeit along slightly different lines. The East Germans' breeding stock came mainly from the Tyrol. Much of their development was along traditional lines and was led and encouraged by a Dr Hofmann. In West Germany the policy differed somewhat and, although the original breeding stock had come from the Tyrol, a great deal of crossbreeding took place including the introduction of a sizeable proportion of Arab blood. The result has been to produce stock which clearly shows the Arabian influence and is tending to move away from some of the more traditional Haflinger attributes, which resulted in Germany giving up its membership of the World Haflinger Federation. Currently, however, the Germans appear to be returning to the traditional breeding principles under the leadership of Dr Dohmen and the standard of their animals is now generally good.

Dr Dohmen, judge at the British Breed Show in 1990, seen with Tom Crane and Whitbourne Scharon, the overall champion.

Dr Dohmen is a respected international judge and has judged at the British Breed Show.

Czech Republic and Slovakia

From the days when these two countries were joined as Czechoslovakia, the timber industry has relied, and still does rely, heavily on horse power. As long ago as the 1930s Haflingers had been introduced for crossbreeding with the native Huzulen horse with the aim of improving the Huzulen. In the late 1950s a number of Haflinger stallions were imported from Austria and there was a great deal of enthusiasm for the Haflinger–Huzulen cross. It was found that in general the desirable Haflinger characteristics did come out in the crossbred ponies and in fact an improvement in the Huzulen was achieved. In late 1993 an approach was made to the Haflinger Society of Great Britain for information on activities with Haflingers by a group of people in Slovakia. They are interested in breeding and promoting Haflingers in the newly established republic and, with the new political openness, enjoy being able to approach whomever they wish.

Switzerland

Haflinger breeding began in Switzerland in the 1940s. The Swiss kept in close contact with the Austrians and followed many of their principles in breeding. The first Swiss breeders' association was formed in 1952 with several more appearing shortly afterward. The Swiss demand for Haflingers was twofold. Army requirements still existed for a packhorse capable of carrying heavy weights and with the stamina for hard work, while another requirement had emerged and was increasing for a horse suitable for leisure pursuits. The Haflinger was able to meet both demands admirably.

Yugoslavia

Sadly today Haflinger breeding in the former Yugoslavia must be affected by the ravages of civil war. However, Yugoslavia was an early convert to the attractions of the Haflinger and breeding began seriously in 1956. The demand was mainly for pack animals and working horses, although some use is made of the Haflinger for riding purposes. Up until the war broke out Yugoslavia had practised a very strict programme of purebreeding and was producing excellent quality Haflingers. What will happen in the future remains to be seen.

Holland

Haflingers first came to Holland in the early 1960s. At that time the demand was for the heavier type of animal, since most of the Dutch breeders were heavy horse experts who had turned to the Haflinger when the need for draught horses decreased and a new requirement appeared for a lighter type than their existing horses, suitable for riding. Early on, the Dutch, like the West Germans, also introduced a considerable amount of Arab blood in an attempt to improve and lighten the stock. However, on joining the World Haflinger Federation in 1986 they opened a separate stud book for Arab crossbreds and they are currently operating a policy of purebreeding. As all the stallions are privately owned, the Dutch breeders' association is not in a position to exercise the same control over breeding as the Austrians do, although they have laid down standards of inspection which must be met before an animal is permitted to be entered in the purebred stud book.

France

The Haflinger stallion, Apollo, together with a number of mares were purchased from the Tyrol in 1964, thus setting France on the Haflinger map. France has followed the

The British stallion Nomad, who was bred in France.

Austrian principles of breeding quite closely and Haflingers are now bred widely throughout the country. The breed society which was quickly formed to maintain standards is *L'Association Française du Poney Haflinger*. In its early days it used to participate actively in the large international agricultural fair held in Paris, much as the British Society introduced the breed at the Royal Show. This advertised and promoted the Haflinger to Frenchmen from all over the country who had travelled to the fair. Much interest was shown and the breed soon gained in popularity. Stallions are privately owned but as well as homebred ones different French breeders have purchased several good quality animals from Austria. The breed society actively promotes purebreeding and will not accept crossbreeding with Arab blood in the main stud book. Today high quality Haflingers are bred in France.

Belgium

In 1966 a Belgian breeder purchased one of the best Haflinger foals at the first foal sale at the *Fohlenhof* and from this small beginning Belgium joined the nations of Haflinger breeders. However, much of the subsequent breeding stock was acquired from her neighbour Holland. Again, with stallions in private ownership, the strict state control over breeding which is exercised by the Austrians is not possible. Belgium has tended in general to follow Holland's lead in most of her breeding activities.

Denmark

It was the early 1970s before Haflingers were first imported into Denmark. However, the breed quickly gained popularity and today two breed societies exist in Denmark. The *Haflingeravlsforeningen Danmark* was founded in the early 1980s and the *Dansk Tyroler Haflinger Avl* was formed in 1986. Denmark is noted for breeding good quality animals and Danish breeders are regular purchasers at the Ebbs auctions. They have in Inge Nobel a respected international judge who has benefited from training with Otto Schweisgut. She was prominent in the establishment of the *Dansk Tyroler Haflinger Avl* whose horses are still occasionally inspected by Otto Schweisgut. Mrs Nobel has purchased stallions from Ebbs and exhibited at the World Haflinger Show.

Albania

Although not a great deal is known about Haflinger breeding activities in this rather remote and enclosed area, it is a fact that Haflingers were introduced into the country in 1968 for the purpose of improving the native breeds. The prime use for horses in Albania is as a working animal for which the Haflinger influence is undoubtedly very suitable, although it is believed that some horses are used for leisure activities.

Sweden

Haflingers have only recently been introduced to Sweden. In 1988 about thirty mares and two stallions were imported. It remains to be seen what use the Swedes will make of them and whether they formulate a breeding policy and become involved with Haflingers on a wider basis.

America

USA

Perhaps surprisingly, the Americans to date have had little influence on Haflinger breeding, although Haflingers were introduced to the USA more than thirty years ago. The first stallion, together with a group of mares, was imported in 1958 by Temple Smith, a wealthy businessman from Illinois. He built up a large stud and for some time was the only serious Haflinger breeder in the States. Of course, in a country as large as the USA it is not as easy to promote the breed widely as it is in smaller countries like those of Europe. However, after Temple Smith's death, his stud was dispersed and the animals were sold to various different parts of the USA, which did produce a wider spread of the breed and attract greater interest in it.

Although Haflingers have now been bred widely throughout the States for a considerable length of time, it is only very recently that the USA has introduced standards for breeding or a system of inspection. Americans do not like to feel that their personal freedom is being curbed in any way and, as a result of differing views on breeding policy, there has been neither any form of selective breeding practised nor a resultant system of inspection. This has meant that anyone could keep their colt as an entire and use it as a stallion, and this practice has led to some poor quality animals being bred. Likewise, there has been no quality control exercised over the mares.

Two breed societies have been established in the USA for some time. In Ohio, where the interest seems to be chiefly in driving activities, a magazine *Haflinger*

Highlite is produced and circulated widely. However, in order to set up a stud book and lay down standards for acceptance, a third society was formed in April 1993 by Raymond and Mim Smith and David and Brenda Villeneuve. It is known as the Haflinger Breeders' Organisation Inc. (HBO) and operates at present in the eastern USA. This society also includes some breeders from eastern Canada.

Much of the work towards achieving the formation of HBO was carried out by Mim Smith, who was already an international judge and committed Haflinger enthusiast. The Austrians have given a great deal of support to the newly formed organisation and until the Americans have sufficient fully trained judges and inspectors, the Tyrolean Haflinger Breeders' Association will carry out the American inspections. Judging at breed shows will only be permitted from qualified Haflinger judges, either in or outside North America, who are members of the World Haflinger Federation. The chief judge of the American Horse Society/American Driving Society, Mim Smith, is already qualified and will continue working with the breed. She also will preside over the HBO judges committee and train other judges in Haflinger judging until the organisation is fully established. Laura Frizzel is also a qualified Haflinger judge.

The first inspections of the newly formed society took place in October 1993 at various locations in eastern USA and Canada. Hannes Schweisgut conducted these inaugural inspections and a large number of yearlings, mares and stallions were graded, using the Austrian 100-point system.

Active efforts are now being made to improve the quality of American breeding stock by importing animals from Europe. American breeder Roy Roney recently visited Britain to purchase stock. The chairman of the British Society, Tom Crane, as well as exporting stock to the USA for a number of years, has also assisted with the setting up of their stud book.

Canada

Haflingers were first introduced to Canada via the USA and later from Europe, including Great Britain. Since 1983 Tom Crane has exported a number of Haflingers to Canada. His connections with the Canadians began when Beth Deslippe came to Britain in the summer of 1983 in search of a yearling or two-year-old colt which could be expected to make the grade as a stallion. After visiting several studs, she selected Majesty, a young M-line colt bred at the Oxnead Stud. In the subsequent years this colt has sired good progeny in both Canada and the USA. Following Majesty's success, the Canadians approached the Cranes again in 1987. On this occasion they purchased six fillies. In 1990 they returned and bought another colt and three more fillies, and also two further youngsters from Ernie Holmes. Canada now possesses some very good breeding stock for whom more than a little credit goes to British animals. In fact, when the consignment of six fillies arrived in Canada, the Canadians remarked that the quality was as good as if not better than some of the stock which had been imported from Austria!

South America

Not a great deal is known about Haflinger activities in South America, but Brazil and Colombia have both imported animals from the Tyrol, whilst Chile and Peru are known to have bought Haflingers from Holland.

Asia

Turkey

In 1961 Turkey imported four stallions and twenty brood mares from Austria and a committed breeding programme began. The Turks' policy is mainly to keep to pure-breds although they have used the Haflinger for crossbreeding with their own native breed, the Karacabey Horse, in an attempt to improve its characteristics. In Turkey, Haflingers have had to adapt to considerable climatic differences from their native environment. Not only are there wide ranges of temperature, but the climate varies in different regions of the country. Although it can snow in winter in the Marmara region, the summers are very hot and dry. Elsewhere, in eastern Turkey winters are very cold and it may snow for several months. Although the winters are somewhat similar to the Haflinger's natural habitat, the hot summers which follow are not. The Haflinger, however, has adapted well and today the breed is firmly established in the country.

Bhutan

The first Haflingers arrived in Bhutan in the Himalayas in 1968. The Haflingers are well suited to the mountainous terrain there and also to the climatic conditions, which are not too dissimilar from those of their native homeland. They are used as pack ponies, for horse transport is often the only means of travelling in this type of region. Haflingers have also been used for crossbreeding with the Tibetan pony with the intention of giving that breed additional stamina and to improve its load-carrying capacity.

India

Because the Haflinger had proved so successful in Bhutan, the Indian Army decided that it would be worth trying them out as army pack ponies. To this end they purchased eight Haflingers in 1980. These animals adapted quickly and well to the conditions, withstanding the altitude and proving fully capable of carrying out all the tasks required of them. Following this trial, a year later a large number of brood mares and working animals were purchased, together with two stallions. India now breeds Haflingers successfully herself and has set strict standards of control with the result that good quality animals are now being produced.

Australia

Haflingers were first imported into Australia by the Dalgety Land Company in 1974. The foundation stock consisted of five brood mares in foal to different stallions, three yearlings and one stallion, Narrogal. In 1980 the stallion Admiral was imported from

Previously champion of Europe, Admiral became champion at the Gold Coast Show (Australia) in 1990.

Barry Paxton-Brown drives Eidelweiss Elani and Eidelweiss Noah (*above*) at exercise and (*below*) as Santa Claus at an Australian Christmas.

Holland where he had previously been European champion. The first Australian-bred Haflinger stallion, Nandewar by Narrogal, was registered in 1986. A W-line stallion, Wintersun, was imported in 1989. By 1994 there were about seventy purebred Haflingers in Australia and probably as many partbreds. In that year the Cranes exported frozen semen from Alpine for artificial insemination. The first crop of Alpine foals was born in Australia in 1995.

The Eidelweiss Stud, one of Australia's major studs, was formed in 1976 by Eve Paxton-Brown in New South Wales. For a number of years she both purchased youngstock from Ebbs and bred her own while actively promoting the Haflinger to the Australians. The stud eventually purchased Admiral before moving in 1988 to Queensland. In 1989 two further mares, both with foals at foot, were purchased from the *Fohlenhof*. In 1990 they went back to Austria briefly to be shown at the International Haflinger Show. The Eidelweiss stud programme follows the Austrian policy of purebreeding.

The show season in Australia takes place during their winter and early spring as it is too hot in their summer. Nevertheless, Haflingers seem to cope with the hot weather without any ill effects, despite having originated from a much colder environment. Admiral has been champion of Australia and other Eidelweiss Haflingers have been successful in various disciplines, in particular driving.

There is a breed society which is known as the Haflinger Horse Society of Australia. Their standards of conformation and temperament are in line with those of the World Haflinger Federation, although the smaller pony still seems to be acceptable. Height for mares ranges from 12.3 hh to 14 hh and for stallions from 13.3 hh to 14.1 hh. Colours ranging from cream to dark chocolate are acceptable, with of course the flaxen manes and tails. The Australians also have a stud book in which all animals passing inspection are registered.

Africa

Little information has been recorded about Haflingers or their activities in Africa. However, it is known that they have been successfully introduced to Namibia where they are used for farming, mainly as a cattle pony. Namibians have also made use of Haflingers as a pack pony for safaris for the tourist trade. As far as is known, the Haflinger has adapted as well here as it has to the other countries where it has been introduced.

And so to the future

What does the future hold for the Haflinger? Almost certainly the Austrians will continue to promote the breed worldwide with enthusiasm. It was originally their native breed and Otto Schweisgut, although now semi-retired, still retains a very keen interest in the future of the Haflinger and continues to maintain and update the stallion genealogical tables of Haflingers worldwide – a task which would be daunting to many a less dedicated person. His son Hannes has now taken the reins at the *Fohlenhof* and is carrying on from where his father left off. In a recent interview given to Friedrich Friedhoff and published in 1995 in the German Haflinger Magazine, Hannes Schweisgut spoke of his aims for the Haflinger of the future. He said the colour will not change and the varying shades of chestnut will continue to be desirable. He considers the current average heights of 14.1 hh for mares and 14.2 hh perhaps even increasing up to 14.3 hh for stallions to be correct. He does not want to see stallions as small as 13.3 hh and says the Austrians will no longer accept stallions of that height. Finally he emphasised the importance of the Haflinger's good temperament and said that under no circumstances should that be permitted to deteriorate.

The World Haflinger Federation will continue to ensure that the standards for breeding and inspection are met and the strong influence of the Austrians is likely to remain, rightly so since the breed is after all native to the Tyrol. Nevertheless, as the Federation encompasses many breeding nations they too will all receive the chance to put their views forward on future policy for breeding.

In Britain, close ties have always been maintained with Austria and the World Haflinger Federation, and will no doubt continue in the future. Of course, within any society members will have differing views and this is so in the Haflinger Society of Great Britain. As we have seen, there is support from some people for what they term the 'old style Haflinger', the smaller chunkier animal which first arrived in Britain in the 1960s. Whether or not this really is the old-style animal is debatable. Early records from Austria indicate that the original Haflingers were around 15 hands in height. It was only during the late 1930s and 1940s that the Haflinger decreased in height, although the effect on breeding stock did continue into the 1960s. Nevertheless, there is still great affection for the stocky pony which first came to Britain. Other members support the Austrians' efforts to produce a taller, finer quality pony, while at the same time retaining the bone substance and other desirable Haflinger attributes.

The first view is largely held by longer-standing members of the Society, many of whom were involved in the early importations of ponies, although some of these members do now support the taller pony. The second view is mainly held by current breeders. Understandably, since they are business people, it is of no use to them if the stock they produce is not readily saleable. The demand is growing for a taller, better quality animal which is suitable for riding by adults. Of course, the shorter stocky type of pony was very rideable but from a point of view of comfort, a taller animal with an improved shoulder giving greater length of stride must give a better ride. Haflingers do tend to be somewhat heavy on their forehand in any case, so attempting also to improve the rear end to enable them to get their hocks under them can surely only be for the better. Activities such as dressage require free-moving, taller animals with better shoulders to execute the more advanced movements. As long as

The modern, taller Haflinger.

the breed is not radically changed, improvements such as are being made are all part of the evolutionary process. Very few breeds run totally unrestricted these days; most breeds are subject to human breeders' requirements, which in turn has an effect on the evolutionary progression, so a future policy and aims of some kind are necessary with any breed.

If standards are not set and maintained, loss of purity would eventually lead to a nondescript rough mongrel of a native pony. However, this is not to say that one should not practise crossbreeding. Used properly, crossbreeding can produce excellent quality animals, although a rather different pony may eventually emerge. Nevertheless, one should always remember that without pure breeds there would not be the purebred stock to use for crossbreeding.

Despite the Austrians' dislike of crossbreeding, I believe that there is a place for it in the Haflinger's future. Of course the first concern must always be to ensure that the purebred animal continues to be of prime importance, but having accepted that, in Britain Haflinger stallions have been put to thoroughbred or part thoroughbred mares and have produced some good quality animals. Likewise, Haflinger mares put to different stallions have bred some good foals. In this country Helen Blair, Zena Fielding, Margaret Davenport and Tom and Susan Crane have experimented with crossbreeding and, in all instances, with good results. The Cranes bred Oxnead Little Louis (out of a Haflinger mare by a thoroughbred stallion) who competed very successfully in top-class company in working hunter pony classes. At one show, judge John Lanni, when selecting him as champion working hunter pony, gave him top marks for jumping, commenting on how well he moved. He said giving full marks was something he had never done before! Helen Blair bred a good quality animal out of a Haflinger mare by an Andalusian stallion, while Margaret Davenport's mare Sisia produced a super pony by a Polish Arab stallion which helped the Oakley Pony Club to the National Tetrathlon title in 1988. Zena Fielding regularly puts her two part thoroughbred mares to Anderson and has bred some excellent foals as a result.

The tendency in crossbreeding seems to be for the Haflinger bone, colour and temperament to combine with the height and finer quality of the thoroughbred (or alternative blood), producing attractive riding animals of around 15 hh to 15.2 hh in the first generation. I am not, however, suggesting that one should continue to breed from crossbreds, since as one moves further away from the purebred, the likelihood is that these animals will become mediocre and nothing positive is then achieved. The currently accepted definition of a Haflinger crossbred is that one parent must be a fully registered Haflinger and the other parent any other registered breed in order for the animal to be accepted in the British Haflinger Partbred Register.

Nelson goes West, ridden by Richard Gillis.

With equestrian activities becoming ever more popular, the Haflinger, with its versatility and adaptability, must have a very bright future in the twenty-first century. It is an all-round family type of horse that is economical to keep, yet incredibly generous in temperament and able to undertake whatever is required of it. As the European Union becomes stronger and the community more closely knit, I would hope that native breeds from all countries will prosper and retain their inherent characteristics and that all will find their place within that union. It would be very sad if any of the individual breeds were lost; they must all be accepted and given equal opportunities. Despite so many enormous changes taking place in the world in less than a century, evolution is a much slower process. Although most of the native ponies have not been truly wild for some considerable time, it is only since the end of the nineteenth or early twentieth century that breed societies have become established and begun to shape the animals' futures in a more organised way. Even with human help, however, the process is still slow and discernable changes and improvements take time to achieve. Therefore the way ahead for the Haflinger, as with most other horses and ponies, must surely be through the breed societies setting and maintaining high standards and encouraging their members to breed animals of the best quality possible, while continuing to promote the ponies actively to the equestrian public.

Bibliography

Haflinger Society of Great Britain, records and Newsletters.

Paul, Winfried, *Haflinger in Europa – Liebe ohne Grenzen*.

Schweisgut, Otto, *Haflinger Horses*. BLV Verlagsgesellschaft mbH, 1988 (English translation).

Schweisgut, Otto, *Der Haflinger das Freizeitpferd aus den Bergen Tirols*. Haflinger Pferdezuchtverband Tirol, 1971.

Schweisgut, Otto, *Haflinger! Ein Pferd erobert die Hertzen der Volker*. Universtatsverlag Wagner, 1965.

Index of horses' names

Page numbers in italics refer to illustrations

Abergele St Patrick (Harry) 47
Adler 32
Adler II 57
Admiral 90, 92
liz. Afghan *31*, 32, 42, 62, 67, 68
Albina-Lucy 68
Aldrian 34
Alex 32
Alpine 64, 65, 66, 67, 76, 92
Anderson 62, 64, 67, 76
Anselmo 21, 30, 31
Apollo 85
Artist 32, 67
Atlas 32
Attila 32

Balmoral Freya 59, 60
Benjo 32
Bergwind 32
Bernhard 32, 46, 52, 63, 64, 65, 67, 76
Berry 57
Bolzano 30
Borga 57, 76
Bozen 32
Brenner 32
Brownbread Story (Merlin) *2*, 47, 48, *78*
Brutus 32, 67

32 Campi 7, 30
Carola 59
Chatsworth Eliza 68
Chatsworth Veronica 68
Chevin Stollen 66, 67, 68, 76
Clifton Brunel 32, 67
Clifton Victoria 68
Coombe Wood Niko 59, 66, 67, 76
Coombe Wood Scharma 59
Coombe Wood Schayla 59

Coombe Wood Schona 59
Coombe Wood Stolz 59, 63, 66, 67, 76
Coombe Wood Strahl 59, 66, 67, 76
Coombe Wood Stumper 59, 67

Devon Adler 62
Devon Novara 62

Edial Mercedes 58
Eger-Elsa 62, 68
Eidelweiss Elani *91*
Eidelweiss Noah *91*
El'Bedavi XXII 1, 6
Evers Patience 68
Evers Schön 59, 68
Evers Schwan 59, 68
Evers Waldchen 61, 67

Foich Linnhe 46
Foich Schiechallion 63
Folie 1, 3, 6, 7, 30, 31
Franzi 59, *60*

Garway Aladdin 64, 76
Garway Orchid 68
54 Genter 8, 31

252/233 Hafling 7, 31
Hafling (Italy) *23*
Heidi I 57
Heidi II 58, 68
Heidrun *45*, 46
Hermi 58, 68
Hety 68

Ilio 33

291 Jenner 8, 31

99

Jeramie 62, 63
Jester 52, 53, 54, 55

Kalterer-Moid 68
Kandida 62, 68, 69

Langford Strida 55
Lispa 59
Lola 59

Magnat 33
Malachi 67
liz.42 Mandl 8, 31
Marika 58, 59
Marius 33, 67
Maserata 43
Massimo 30, 32
Maximilian 61, 67, 76
Meteor 33
Midas 33
Mölten 33
Monar 62, 67
Mordskerl 33, 67

Nandewar 92
Narrogal 90, 92
Nautilus 34
liz. Naz 33, 34
Nelson 65, 66, 67, 77, *96*
New Yorker 68
Nibbio 30, 33
Nilo 32, 33, 67
Nina 68
Nomad 49, 64, 66, 67, 76, *85*
Norden 34
Notangus 57
Notker 57

Olfa 62, 68
Olwyn 68
Oxnead Adam 64
Oxnead Alpha 64, 77
Oxnead Ambassador 67, 68
Oxnead Aristocrat *48*, 49, 66, 67, 68, 76, *77*

Oxnead Little Louis 95
Oxnead Majesty 67, 88
Oxnead Nania 68
Oxnead Natalie 68
Oxnead Nobell 68
Oxnead Sadie 59
Oxnead Sapphire 59
Oxnead Signoretta 59

Pendavey Matra 52
Putz 61, 67, 68

Ridi 59

Salurn 34
Salut 34
Saturn 34
Schatzel 59, 68
Silber 34
Silbersee 34, 38
Silverton Noury 68
Silverton Oriana 68
Silverton Ottilia *19*, 68
Sisia 59, 95
Sissi 57
Sitka 53, 70
Solfried 49, 52
Steiger 34
Steinadler 35, 62, 67
Stelvio 30, 34
Stern 34
Stolz 34
Stormer 61, 66, 67, 76
Strom 34, 67
Stromer 34, 67
Strudl 62, 66, 67, 76
Stuart 42
Stüber 34, *35*, 68
Student 30, 34
Stürmer 34, 42
liz. Stürmer 33, 67, 69
Sturmwind 34

Texas 61

100

Tilly 57
Trista 59, *60*

Udina 57

Verena 61, 68

Waldo 59
Wardein 35, 36
Westwind 61, 67
Whitbourne Scharon *83*
Wieland 35, 37

Wildmoos 36
Wilfried 35
liz. Willi 31, 35, *36*
Willi I 35
Wilten 36
Winchester 36
Winterstein 67
Wintersun 92
Wirbel 36
Wrekin Helga 68
Wrekin Storli *79*